PRUNING
BASICS

PRUNING
BASICS

David Squire

Sterling Publishing Co., Inc.
New York

Library of Congress Cataloging-in-Publication Data
Available

10 9 8 7 6 5 4 3 2 1

Published by Sterling Publishing Company, Inc.
387 Park Avenue South, New York, NY 10016
First published in Great Britain by Hamlyn,
a division of Octopus Publishing Group Limited

© 2001 Octopus Publishing Group Limited

Distributed in Canada by Sterling Publishing
c/o Canadian Manda Group, One Atlantic Avenue,
Suite 105, Toronto, Ontario, Canada M6K 3E7

Printed in China
Sterling ISBN 0-8069-5113-3

CONTENTS

INTRODUCTION

Gardeners have seldom been content to leave the growth of plants solely to the vagaries of nature. Rather, they are shapers of their environment, experimenting with the removal of parts of plants to encourage the development of larger and better fruits and flowers, more colourful leaves and stems, or more shapely or compact plants. Pruning is the means by which they seek to achieve these ends.

Few gardening techniques have been cloaked in as much mystique as pruning, yet basically it is a simple and logical process. In temperate countries its timing is strongly influenced by the onset and retreat of winter weather that would damage young shoots. Tropical and subtropical regions also have their own growth-limiting influences, particularly droughts, both seasonal and prolonged.

In this practical step-by-step book, we deal only with pruning the range of trees, shrubs and fruits that are widely grown in temperate regions. Ornamental shrubs and trees create varied shapes and colours, and range from low-growing heathers to flowering trees and shrubs, many with coloured leaves or stems. Some need only the flowers to be lightly clipped off, while with others whole stems and shoots are removed. The specific pruning needs of each group are explained in detail. Also included are a number of techniques, such as bark-ringing and root-pruning, that are now less widely practised since the introduction of many less vigorous and more predictable rootstocks. These techniques are, nevertheless, described because many older gardens have large, unfruitful trees that pre-date these developments.

It is important to bear in mind that pruning is not, essentially, a way to keep a shrub, tree or conifer small. Bonsai, a specialized method of pruning that restricts growth, is a technique that is suitable only for plants that are grown in shallow pots. Such plants require specialist treatment, including leaf stripping and clipping and root-pruning, and this is not the subject of this book. You should never, therefore, knowingly buy a plant that will eventually become too large for your garden.

Above: Pruning is essential
to keep many garden plants
compact, shapely and
flowering in profusion.

Left: Roses need to be pruned regularly to provide a stunning display each year.
Below: *Taxus baccata* (yew) needs pruning to maintain a neat shape and promote new growth.

why prune?

Botanical purists might argue that even grass needs pruning to keep it at a uniform height and to encourage the development, in certain species, of shoots from the base. It is, however, woody plants that are the prime candidates for pruning, and these come in the form of ornamental shrubs and trees (including conifers), fruit trees, bushes and canes, climbers, hedges and topiary. Roses, which enjoy something of a cult status, are deciduous flowering shrubs that need regular pruning to keep them healthy and capable of creating a radiant display each year. Pruning roses is more complex than pruning most other shrubs because there are so many different types. Their pruning is also influenced by the type of soil, whether the plant is newly planted or established, and whether it is being grown for exhibition or just for display in the garden. Throughout this book these and other variations are illustrated and explained, and

roses are considered separately from other deciduous shrubs.

Nature has produced shrubs and trees with such a wide range of habits that it is not surprising that pruning techniques vary widely, both in the time of year pruning is best performed and the type of shoots that are removed. Frequently plants within the same genus have different needs. For example, most *Aesculus* spp. (horse chestnuts) grow into trees that are too large for planting in gardens, but *A. parviflora* (bottlebrush buckeye) has a suckering nature, with shoots growing from ground level. With this species, encouraging the development of fresh shoots from the ground is important, whereas species grown as trees need little pruning other than being shaped when young.

When shrubs have not been regularly pruned, they age prematurely and do not create a good display. Some may grow too large, obscuring other plants,

blocking out light and draining the soil of moisture and nutrients, to the detriment of nearby plants.

If you inherit a garden full of large or neglected plants, do not rip them out straight away before considering whether they can be cut back to encourage the development of new growth from the base. Some shrubs can be rejuvenated by spreading the pruning over two or three years. In addition, feeding shrubs that have been severely pruned encourages the development of fresh shoots. Those that are a jungle of gnarled branches or thin, bare stems should, however, be replaced with young specimens, but remember to improve the soil first.

FLOWERING SHRUBS
Shrubs are among the most popular garden plants. When they are correctly pruned they will produce colourful flowers that will last for several weeks every year. Some create their display in spring or summer; others in winter when there is a lack of colour. A few shrubs, such as *Cornus alba* (red-barked

dogwood), are specifically grown for their colourful stems, which brighten gardens in winter and early spring. Other shrubs are grown for their colourful leaves; this group includes variegated and evergreen hollies (*Ilex* spp.), as well as deciduous shrubs, such as *Philadelphus coronarius* 'Aureus', which develop fresh foliage each spring.

Many deciduous shrubs are popular for their rich autumn leaf colours, which daily grow brighter and more attractive until the leaves fall in late autumn or early winter. Berries are an important feature of some shrubs and trees and help to brighten gardens from autumn through to late winter.

TREES

Trees require less regular pruning than shrubs, although during their formative years it is essential that crossing branches are removed. Most deciduous trees are pruned in winter when they are dormant. Flowering cherries and other members of the *Prunus* genus, however, must be pruned in spring or early summer, when their sap is rising, to prevent the entry of diseases such as bacterial canker.

HEDGES AND TOPIARY

Hedges are an important part of gardens. Dense evergreen or coniferous hedges are especially valuable at the perimeter to make windbreaks or provide privacy. They need pruning to create attractive shapes. Small flowering shrubs used to separate one part of the garden from another are pruned to promote regular flowering.

Pruning deciduous hedges helps to produce a mass of shoots from their base: hedges with thin bases are always an eyesore.

The art of topiary was known to the Romans in the first century AD. In the following centuries its popularity waned, although in the Middle Ages plants were trained, clipped and tied to flexible stems. Nowadays, most garden topiary is formed from *Taxus baccata* (common yew), *Buxus sempervirens* 'Suffruticosa' (edging box) and *Lonicera nitida* (shrubby honeysuckle).

FRUIT TREES, BUSHES AND CANES

Fruit trees, bushes and cane fruits need regular pruning to encourage the yearly production of good-sized, healthy fruits. Pruning also helps to ensure that trees do not become congested with shoots and age prematurely. Apples and pears grow in a variety of forms, including

bushes, trees, pyramids, cordons and espaliers. The nature of bush-grown soft fruits varies widely – blackcurrants develop fruits on shoots produced in the previous year, for example, while redcurrants and whitecurrants, together with gooseberries, have a more permanent framework. Cane fruits, such as raspberries, develop fresh canes each year. Canes that have produced fruits should be removed immediately the crop is picked.

GRAPE VINES

Grape vines are among the oldest cultivated plants. Pruning the woody structure is essential for the development of grapes as well as the training of the vine. Another part of pruning is thinning the fruits, to ensure that the fruits that remain reach a good size. There are several ways to prune grapes, but they all encourage the development of young shoots each year.

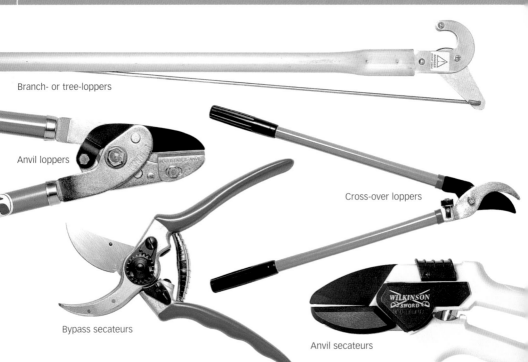

Branch- or tree-loppers

Anvil loppers

Cross-over loppers

Bypass secateurs

Anvil secateurs

tools

Pruning tools should be functional as well as pleasant and easy to use. Always handle a tool before buying it, making sure that it fits your hand and feels comfortable, and always buy the best-quality tools you can afford as invariably these last longer than less expensive, inferior models. Pruning tools must be kept sharp if they are to function easily and successfully. Clean and wipe them after use and, if they are not to be used for a few weeks, lightly oil metal parts.

Electrically powered tools are especially dangerous if they are not used responsibly. Always install a circuit-breaking device to make sure that the power is cut off should the cable be severed or a fault occur with the tool. At the end of each season, have the equipment serviced by a competent electrician and replace all worn cables. Carefully inspect all plugs and sockets in the interest of safety.

Secateurs are available in two basic forms. The bypass model (also known as cross-over or parrot type) has a scissor-like action and cuts when one blade passes the other. The other is an anvil type, with a sharp blade that cuts when in contact with a firm, flat, metal surface known as an anvil. Both types come in several sizes. Most secateurs are sold to suit right-handed people, but left-handed models are also available.

Branch- or tree-loppers are ideal for cutting shoots high on fruit trees. They cut shoots up to 2–3cm (1in) thick and from branches 3m (l0ft) high. They are ideal for pruning large and vigorous fruit trees that have been neglected or those grafted on to too-vigorous rootstocks. Do not use loppers to cut exceptionally thick or tough shoots as this will blunt the blades. After thick branches have been removed, cover any cut surfaces with a liberal coating of fungicidal wound paint to prevent

any disease or infection from entering the tree. Use an old brush for this.

Loppers have long handles and make it possible to remove thick shoots without having to use a saw. There are two types of cutting action, cross-over and anvil. Most loppers have handles 38–45cm (15–18in) long and cut wood to 3.5cm (1½in) thick. Heavy-duty loppers, with handles 75cm (30in) long, cut wood 5cm (2in) thick. Some anvil types have a compound cutting action that enables thick branches to be cut with greater ease. Although loppers are quick and easy to use, they are soon strained if used continuously to cut excessively thick and tough shoots.

Folding saws are ideal for carrying in a pocket and are usually 18cm (7in) when folded, extending to 40cm (16in) long in use. Other models have 23cm (9in) long blades and extend to 55cm (22in) when unfolded. The teeth cut on both the push and pull strokes. Most folding saws cut wood 3.5cm (1½in) thick. Replacement blades are available for most models.

Straight-bladed, fixed-handled saws are usually able to cut branches 13cm (5in) thick, although high-specification ones sever branches 18cm (7in) thick. Blade lengths range from 25 to 30cm (10–12in). Replacement blades are available.

Saws with curved blades, sometimes known as Grecian saws, cut on the pull stroke. Because the blade is tapered and pointed, the saw is usable in confined spaces.

Bow saws are usually 60–90cm (2–3ft) long, although some are only 30cm (12in). The blade is kept under tension by a lever.

Knives were once used by professional gardeners to prune shrubs and fruit trees, but, unless the blade is exceptionally sharp and unless you are experienced, both plants and hands become damaged. Pruning knives are now mainly reserved for paring cut surfaces smooth before an application of a fungicidal wound paint. They are, however, essential for bark-ringing trunks or notching and nicking buds. Knives are available in many sizes, with blades that fold into the handle. It is false economy to buy a cheap knife because the blade will need repeated sharpening and may not be strongly secured in the handle.

Hand shears are ideal for trimming hedges and beds of heathers. Most models will cut stems up to the thickness of a pencil. Some have a notch near the base of each blade to enable thicker shoots to be severed. Rubber-clad handles absorb the wrist-juddering action of repeated opening and closing.

Powered hedge clippers are essential where there is extensive hedging. Petrol-powered generators that power electrical hedge clippers are ideal in areas far away from power supplies. Cordless models cut about 83sq m (100sq yards) of hedging between recharges from a mains electricity supply. Most types are powered by mains electricity, however. Cutting blades range in length from 33 to 75cm (13–30in), and although a few have cutting knives on one side only others have knives on both and are therefore usable by either left- or right-handed gardeners.

Straight-bladed, fixed-handled saw

Bow saw

Saw with curved blade

Folding saw

Hand shears

Powered hedge clippers

1 SHRUBS

Ornamental shrubs create the framework of a garden, around which herbaceous perennials, annuals, biennials and rock-garden plants can be featured. These woody plants are, with trees, the most permanent features of a garden, and they therefore need careful training and pruning, especially during the early years. The pruning they require varies enormously. Coniferous plants, once established, need little attention, but deciduous and evergreen shrubs should be checked every year, if only to make sure that the centres are not becoming congested with crossing stems and excessive growth.

Left: Philadelphus species (mock orange) are grown for their fragrant flowers which are produced in summer.
Above: Ceanothus arboreus 'Trewithin Blue' growing against a wall provides a splash of blue in the garden in early summer.

Deciduous shrubs shed their leaves in autumn and develop fresh ones in spring. This enables them to survive winter in a dormant state without suffering appreciable damage, while retaining the ability to continue growth with a fresh set of leaves in spring. In severe winters the tips of immature shoots may be damaged, but survival is usually assured unless the shrub is exceptionally tender. Not all deciduous shrubs need annual pruning, but those that do can be divided into three types according to their flowering time: 'winter', 'spring to midsummer' and 'late summer'. Evergreen shrubs retain their leaves all year round, of course, and often require less pruning than deciduous species. Nevertheless, flowering evergreen plants such as *Lavandula* spp. (lavender) have different requirements from *Erica* spp. and *Calluna* spp. (heathers).

Before pruning any shrub it is essential to know its name: the nature and flowering times of shrubs can vary widely, even within a genus and between species. *Buddleja davidii* (butterfly bush), for example, flowers from mid- to late summer, while *B. alternifolia* creates its display in early summer. *Viburnum* x *bodnantense* flowers from late autumn to early spring, while the fragrant flowers of *V. japonicum* are borne in summer. It is a good idea to make sure that plants are correctly labelled or recorded in a notebook so that you can double-check that you are cutting back the correct plant at the correct time.

Many of the ornamental shrubs, both deciduous and evergreen, discussed in this section are also suitable for use as informal or formal hedges, and many species are described on pages 74–85. The main difference is that hedging plants are usually cut back harder than specimen plants grown in the border. The deciduous shrubs that are described on the following pages are categorized by flowering period; this will, of course, vary according to the climate and the micro-climate in your own garden.

Whatever pruning group a shrub is in, always clear away and burn pruned wood in case the shrub is infected with diseases or harbours pests. In this way you can be sure that any infection or pests will not spread to other plants. It is not usually necessary to apply wound paint to cuts on shrubs. Provided all pruning is carried out with sharp secateurs and the cuts are made cleanly, there is no need to apply wound paint. A callus will form quickly on a clean cut on a slender branch.

deciduous shrubs

In temperate countries, where each year the temperature falls in autumn or early winter and plants are exposed to frosts, deciduous flowering shrubs can be divided into three groups.

Winter- and early spring-flowering types, which require little pruning and are pruned immediately their flowers fade. This group includes plants such as *Hamamelis mollis* (Chinese witch hazel), which bears golden-yellow flowers in mid- and late winter, and *Cornus mas* (cornelian cherry), which bears umbels of yellow flowers in late winter.

Mid-spring- to midsummer-flowering shrubs form a second group and are pruned as soon as their flowers fade, so that young growth encouraged by pruning has time to ripen and harden before the onset of winter. This group includes plants such as *Deutzia* spp., *Kolkwitzia amabilis* (beauty bush) and *Weigela* spp.

Late summer- and autumn-flowering shrubs are included in a third group. For shrubs in this category pruning is delayed until spring of the following year, when they will be free from the risk of frost damage. Plants in this group include hardy fuchsias, deciduous *Ceanothus* spp. and *Spiraea japonica*.

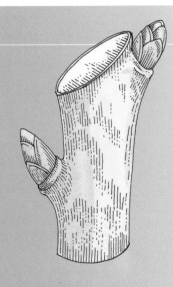

Pruning cuts

*The position of a cut in relation to a bud is important and influences subsequent growth. The illustration on the left shows the correct position of a cut: slightly sloping, with the upper point just above a bud. If the cut slopes downwards and towards the bud (**a**), there is a danger that it might be damaged. If the cut is too high (**b**), the stub will die back and allow diseases to enter. Cuts that are positioned extremely close to the bud (**c**) may leave the bud unsupported and damaged.*

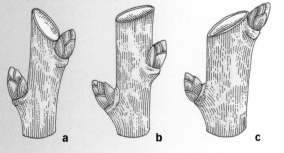

a   b   c

The general principles of pruning these shrubs are described here, but there are many specific variations and these are detailed on pages 16–23. Variations include leaving on the old flowerheads of *Hydrangea macrophylla*, which bears flowers in midsummer and into autumn, until spring of the following year, when the old shoots are removed to leave young ones that will bear flowers later in the year. Leaving the old flowerheads in position in winter protects the shoots, as well as providing areas on which frost can create attractive patterns.

The grouping of flowering deciduous shrubs into three groups is based on the expectation that from late spring or early summer the weather will be free from frost. In reality, however, there are considerable differences in the severity of weather and the date of the last frost in spring or early summer. The local climate must therefore be taken into consideration; freezing temperatures might damage freshly developed young shoots in early summer. In areas that rarely experience frost, pruning can be performed safely in late winter. If you are in any doubt about the severity and timing of frosts in your area you could consult the meteorological office. Alternatively, local horticultural clubs or gardening associations often have a very good idea of the micro-climates in particular areas.

Old, neglected deciduous shrubs sometimes become covered in algae. Renovation pruning will remove much of this, but any algae that is left can be removed by spraying with a winter-wash (the type used for apple and pear trees). Use this only when the shrub is dormant and free from leaves, and make sure that late winter- and spring-flowering bulbs planted under and around deciduous shrubs have not appeared above the soil's surface. Take care when treading on soil, as the shoots of bulbs may be just below the surface and can be easily damaged. Shoots from early-developing herbaceous plants will also be damaged if the soil's surface is walked on.

Left: *Hamamelis mollis* (Chinese witch hazel) is a winter-flowering deciduous shrub that requires little pruning.
Below: After the flowers of *Kolkwitzia amabilis* (beauty bush) have faded in early summer, cut out flowered shoots to encourage new growth.

Left: *Viburnum opulus* 'Compactum' has white flowers in spring and early summer followed by bunches of bright red berries. Thin out crowded branches in midsummer. *Below*: Prune *Forsythia* x *intermedia* 'Week End' (golden bells) after the flowers have faded in spring.

deciduous shrubs:
winter- & early spring-flowering shrubs

Winter colour

Many shrubs are grown for their attractive stems, which provide colour in winter borders. These shrubs include Cornus alba *(common dogwood)*, C. stolonifera *(syn.* C. sericea; red osier dogwood) *and* C. stolonifera *'Flaviramea'. In spring use loppers to cut down all stems to within 5–8cm (2–3in) of the ground. This encourages the development of fresh stems that will create a bright feature in winter.*

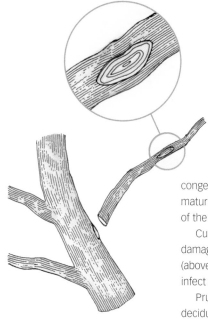

CARE OF WINTER-FLOWERING SHRUBS

Winter-flowering deciduous shrubs need little pruning other than shaping when young and the removal of branches that cross the plant's centre, creating congestion and reducing the maturing and ripening influence of the sun.

Cut out pest- and disease-damaged shoots at the base (above); if left, the decay may infect and damage other parts.

Prune winter-flowering deciduous shrubs once their display is over. This gives the maximum time to produce new shoots and for them to ripen before the onset of cold weather in the following autumn or early winter. It is easier to control the size of winter-flowering shrubs than any other type.

Suggested plants

Abeliophyllum distichum **(white forsythia)** is an early-flowering deciduous shrub that needs little pruning, other than the cutting out of dead shoots in spring. In cold areas leave pruning until early summer. Scented, pink-tinged white flowers are borne in late winter to early spring.

Corylopsis **spp. (winter hazel)** have racemes of fragrant yellow flowers in early spring, before the leaves appear. No regular pruning is needed, other than occasionally thinning out crowded shoots after the flowers have faded.

Forsythia **spp. (golden bells)** are one of the joys of early spring. There are several species and varieties , but *F.* x *intermedia* 'Spectabilis' is one of the best, with bright yellow, bell-shaped flowers. *F.* x *intermedia* 'Lynwood' has even larger, rich yellow flowers. Prune annually after the flowers have faded in spring. Cut out straggly and misplaced shoots and shorten long and vigorous stems. If pruning is neglected, the shrub becomes choked with old wood, reducing the number of flowering shoots.

Hamamelis **spp. (witch hazel)** requires no regular pruning, but cut back straggly, diseased, crowded or crossing shoots in late winter or spring. *H. mollis* (Chinese witch hazel), which grows to 2.4m (8ft) high and wide, bears spider-like, sweetly scented, golden-yellow flowers in winter. In autumn this deciduous shrub has mid-green leaves that assume yellow tints before falling.

Stachyurus chinensis is a spreading shrub, bearing pale yellow, bell-like flowers on arching stems in late winter to early spring. No regular pruning is needed, but occasionally shorten long shoots in mid-spring to maintain the shape.

Viburnum is a large genus, that includes some winter-flowering deciduous species. No regular pruning is needed for deciduous species, other than occasionally cutting out crowded branches after the flowers have faded in spring.

Left: Weigela 'Eva Rathke'bears pretty crimson flowers in early summer. *Below: Sambucus racemosa* 'Sutherland Gold' (elder) has colourful, feathery foliage. For best foliage effect, cut all the stems to ground level in spring.

deciduous shrubs:
early-flowering shrubs

CARING FOR EARLY-FLOWERING SHRUBS

Prune early-flowering deciduous shrubs, flowering between mid-spring and midsummer, as soon as their flowers fade.

First, cut out thin and weak shoots and those that cross a shrub's centre. Then, cut out to within a couple of buds of their base all shoots that have borne flowers. The removal of flowered shoots leaves young ones that will bear flowers in the following year. If shrubs have been neglected for several seasons, many can be rejuvenated by cutting back the complete shrub. However, this usually means foregoing flowers for one season.

suggested plants

Amelanchier lamarckii (snowy mespilus) bears a mass of pure white, star-like flowers in large, loose clusters in mid-spring. In autumn, the green leaves, which are coppery when young, assume rich yellow and orange tints. In late summer it develops red fruits that slowly become purple or black. It eventually forms a shrub to 3m (10ft) high. Little pruning is needed, but thin out overcrowded bushes in early summer, after the flowers fade. *A. canadensis* and *A. laevis* are pruned in the same manner.

Buddleja globosa (orange ball tree) should be pruned immediately after the flowers fade in early summer. Cut out the dead flowers and 5–8cm (2–-3in) of the old wood.

Caragana arborescens (Siberian pea tree) needs no regular pruning, but long growths on young plants should be carefully shortened after the flowers fade.

Cytisus x praecox (Warminster broom) is a deciduous shrub with a bushy, vigorous habit, growing to 1.8m (6ft). The arching stems bear creamy-white, pea-shaped flowers in mid- and late spring. The cultivar 'Allgold' has bright yellow flowers, which look spectacular but have a rather acrid smell. Make sure that young plants become bushy by trimming off leading shoots during the first summer. When established, prune *Cytisus* plants that flower on the previous season's shoots as soon as the flowers have faded, removing two-thirds off all shoots. Other *Cytisus* that flower on the current season's growth are pruned in spring, cutting shoots hard back before growth recommences.

Deutzia spp. are attractive deciduous shrubs, bearing white or pale pink flowers from mid-spring to midsummer. Cut out all flowered shoots to their bases as soon as the flowers have faded in midsummer.

Dipelta floribunda is a multi-stemmed shrub, to about 4m (12ft). After the flowers have faded in early or midsummer, cut a few of the old stems to ground level to keep the bushes open and to encourage the development of further shoots.

Enkianthus campanulatus, which bears pink-veined yellow flowers in late spring, just needs its shape maintained in late winter.

Fothergilla spp. need no regular pruning, other than occasionally thinning out overcrowded and twiggy shoots after the flowers have faded in late spring or early summer. *F. major* is a North American shrub, about 2.4m (8ft) high and 1.8m (6ft) across. It bears sweetly scented, creamy-white flowers like bottle-brushes in late spring. In autumn the dark-green leaves develop red or orange-yellow tints.

Hippophae rhamnoides (sea buckthorn), which has tiny yellowish-green flowers in spring, needs no regular pruning, but cut out straggly shoots in late summer.

Kerria japonica (Jew's mallow, Japanese rose) is a strongly suckering shrub. In late spring and early summer it bears yellow-orange flowers. The form 'Pleniflora' has double flowers to 5cm (2in) across and is commonly known as bachelor's buttons, and it is slightly more vigorous than the single-flowered species. Both usually grow to 1.2–1.8m (4–6ft). After the flowers have faded, cut out the old wood to strong, new growths. Alternatively, sever them at soil level to encourage the development of strong growths from the shrub's base.

Kolkwitzia amabilis (beauty bush) creates a magnificent display in late spring and early summer. Clusters of pink, foxglove-like flowers with yellow throats adorn the ends of twiggy stems. It has an upright habit, with arching branches, and grows to 2.4–3m (8–10ft) high. After the flowers have faded in early summer, completely cut out flowered shoots to encourage fresh growth.

Paeonia suffruticosa (moutan, tree peony) grows to about 2.1m (7ft) high. No regular pruning is needed other than to cut out dead shoots in spring and to remove seedpods as soon as the flowers fall.

Perovskia atriplicifolia (Russian sage) has attractive grey foliage and blue flowers. In mid-spring cut all shoots to 30cm (12in) high to encourage the development of fresh shoots. In cold areas leave pruning until all risk of severe frost has passed.

Sambucus spp. (elder) are vigorous deciduous shrubs. Thin out bushes in mid-spring to keep them neat and shapely. Where forms such as *S. racemosa* 'Plumosa Aurea' and *S. nigra* 'Aureomarginata' are grown for their colourful leaves, cut all the stems back to ground level each spring.

Spiraea is a genus of about 80 shrubs, some of which are semi-evergreen, although most are deciduous. *S.* 'Arguta' (syn. *S. x arguta* 'Bridal Wreath') becomes smothered in 5cm (2in) wide clusters of white flowers in mid- and late spring. It is a superb deciduous shrub, ideal for shrub borders as well as next to paths and boundaries. Other spring-flowering species include *S. thunbergii*, which has 2.5cm (1in) wide clusters of white flowers, and *S. x vanhouttei*, which has dense clusters of white flowers during early summer. On young and semi-mature shrubs, cut back flowering shoots as soon as the flowers have faded, leaving one or two young shoots at the base of each shoot. As a shrub develops, cut out as much of the old wood as possible in late winter, leaving the previous year's growth to produce flowers during the current year. On *S. japonica* and *S. japonica* 'Bumalda' prune all stems to within 8–10cm (3–4in) of the ground in late winter or early spring.

Staphylea spp. (bladdernut) need no regular pruning, but occasionally cut back long growths after the flowers have faded in late spring.

Stephanandra spp. are similar to *Spiraea*. Cut out old and spindly shoots in late winter or early summer.

Weigela cultivars are deciduous shrubs with small, foxglove-like flowers, which are borne in early summer. The cultivars grow to 1.5-1.8m (5-6ft) high. In addition to varieties grown for their flowers, *W.* 'Florida Variegata' has mid-green leaves with creamy-white edges. *W.* 'Eva Rathke' has crimson flowers. Each year, after the flowers have faded in midsummer, cut out to soil level a few of the old stems. If this is neglected, the shrub soon becomes a tangled web of old shoots that produce only small and inferior flowers.

Left: *Cistus creticus* subsp. *incanus* is an evergreen, bushy shrub which bears striking purplish-pink flowers throughout summer. *Right*: *Philadelphus* 'Dame Blanche' has an elegant combination of dark green foliage and loose white flowers which are borne in profusion from early to midsummer.

deciduous shrubs:
late-flowering shrubs

CARE OF LATE-FLOWERING SHRUBS

Late-flowering deciduous shrubs, bearing flowers in late summer or autumn, are pruned in late spring of the following year. If they are pruned immediately after their flowers fade, the young shoots that subsequently develop would be damaged by frosts in winter. By leaving pruning until the following year, the fresh young shoots will not be exposed to frost.

First, cut out dead and diseased shoots, then those that cross the centre of the shrub. At the same time, cut out thin and weak shoots. Next, cut to just above a bud all those shoots that produced flowers in the previous year. Pruning varies slightly according to the individual shrubs, and some are listed on pages 22–3.

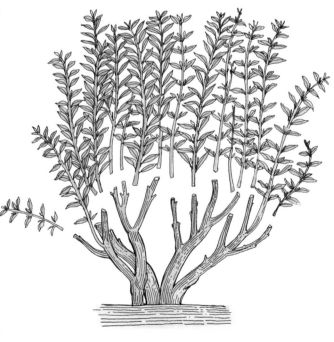

Pruning hydrangeas

Hydrangea macrophylla *(mop-head hydrangeas)* are superb garden shrubs, which flower from midsummer right through into autumn. Leave the flower stems and old flowerheads in place until late winter or early spring. Then, cut out all shoots that produced flowers in the previous year. This radically thins out the shrub, allows light and air to enter, and encourages the development of fresh shoots which will bear flowers later in the year.

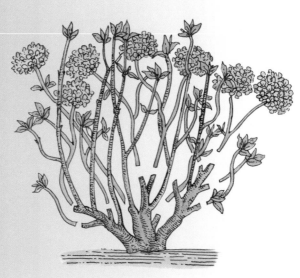

suggested plants

Aesculus parviflora (bottlebrush buckeye) is a suckering shrub. Cut out congested, old stems at ground level in late summer or early autumn to encourage the development of fresh ones. If pruning is left until spring there is a risk that the plant will bleed. This applies to all members of the horse chestnut family.

Artemisia abrotanum (lad's love, southernwood) is semi-evergreen in mild areas. Cut out frosted and congested shoots in early spring.

Buddleja is a genus of about 100 deciduous, evergreen and semi-evergreen species. As soon as the flowers of *B. alternifolia* fade in the latter part of early summer, cut back by two-thirds all the stems that produced flowers. This prevents the shrub from becoming congested with old shoots. *B. davidii* (butterfly bush) needs regular pruning in early spring. Cut back all the previous season's shoots to within 5–8cm (2–3in) of the older wood. This encourages the development of fresh shoots that will bear flowers later in the same year.

Callicarpa dichotoma During early and mid-spring, thin out overcrowded bushes, retaining as much of the young, healthy wood as possible.

Calycanthus spp. (allspice) have fragrant flowers, borne on the current year's growth. In spring thin out overcrowded bushes, taking care to retain as much of the young and healthy wood as possible.

Caryopteris x clandonensis (bluebeard) bears blue flowers in late summer. In early spring cut back shoots produced during the previous year – weak shoots to soil level and stronger ones to healthy buds. This encourages the development of fresh shoots from ground level.

Ceanothus spp. can be evergreen or deciduous. Prune late summer- and autumn-flowering deciduous types in spring, cutting thin shoots and pruning strong stems that produced flowers the previous year to 15–30cm (6–I2in) from old wood.

Ceratostigma willmottianum (shrubby plumbago, Chinese plumbago) is a slightly tender shrub, with lovely pale blue flowers, borne in terminal clusters, in mid- to late summer. The diamond-shaped, dark-green leaves assume reddish tints in autumn. In temperate regions shoots are often killed by frost. If this happens cut the whole plant to ground level in mid-spring to encourage new stems and flowers. If shoots are not damaged by frost, just cut out old, flowered ones.

Chimonanthus praecox (wintersweet) requires little attention when grown as a bush in a border, other than to thin shoots in spring. When it is grown against a wall, cut out flowered shoots to within two buds of their base after the yellow, spicy-scented flowers have faded.

Chionanthus virginicus (fringe tree) is a deciduous shrub or small tree to 3m (10ft). After the flowers fade in midsummer, thin crowded bushes by cutting out weak and spindly shoots.

Cistus cvs (rock rose) are grown for their showy flowers, which are borne throughout summer. When plants are young, nip out the growing points from young shoots to encourage the development of bushy plants. When fully grown these plants dislike being pruned. If old wood is cut, fresh shoots do not develop from it. Old, leggy, unsightly plants are best dug up and replaced.

Clerodendrum bungei (glory flower) and *C. trichotomum* are slightly tender shrubs that need little pruning, other than cutting out the tips of any frost-damaged shoots in spring. When plants become large, cut them to within 30–35cm (12–15in) of the base in spring.

Clethra alnifolia (sweet pepper bush) forms a deciduous shrub with fragrant, bell-shaped, creamy-white flowers in late summer and into autumn. The cultivar 'Pink Spire' has pretty pink flowers. *C. arborea* (lily-of-the-valley tree) has very fragrant white flowers, also in late summer to mid-autumn. No regular pruning is needed, other than to cut out old shoots and remove thin and weak wood during winter and early spring.

Genista spp. (broom) need no regular pruning, but encourage bushiness in young plants by nipping out the tips of shoots.

Hibiscus syriacus (shrubby althaea, shrubby mallow) needs no regular pruning, but shorten long shoots in spring.

Hydrangea is a genus of about 80 species, including some evergreens and climbers. Most are deciduous shrubby plants. *H. arborescens* (sevenbark) grows to 2.4m (8ft) and bears corymbs of white flowers. In late winter or early spring cut back by

Bottom left: Prune *Buddleja davidii* 'Harlequin' (butterfly bush) regularly in early spring to encourage the development of new shoots.

Right: The long shoots of *Hibiscus syriacus* 'Red Heart' (shrubby mallow) should be shortened in spring.

a third to a half all shoots that produced flowers during the previous year. There are two forms of *H. macrophylla*, lacecap and hortensia. It is usually dome-shaped and 1.2–1.8m (4–6ft) high, with flowers from midsummer to autumn. In late winter or early spring, cut out by half all shoots that produced flowers during the previous year. The old flowerheads are removed in autumn, but leaving them in place until spring helps to provide protection for the plant when it is grown in a cold climate.

Indigofera decora is a tender shrub bearing red-flushed, white flowers. No regular pruning is needed, but cut out frost-damaged shoots in early spring. If shrubs become overcrowded and too large or are severely damaged by frost, cut all shoots almost to ground level in late spring.

Leycesteria formosa (Himalayan honeysuckle) is an upright shrub, bearing white flowers and purple bracts. In spring cut out to ground level all shoots that produced flowers during the previous year.

Philadelphus spp. (mock orange) are grown for their fragrant flowers. After the flowers fade cut out all shoots that produced flowers. Leave young shoots, as these will produce flowers during the following year.

Potentilla fruticosa and **P. fruticosa** var. **arbuscula (cinquefoil)** bear flowers over a long period in summer and autumn. They need little pruning, but cut out straggly, old and weak shoots at the bases after the flowers have faded.

Rhus spp. (sumach) do not usually require regular pruning, but if a mass of foliage is required cut all stems of *R. typhina*, *R. typhina* 'Dissecta' and *R. glabra* to the ground each year

between late winter and mid-spring. In cold areas leave pruning until late spring.

Romneya coulteri (matilija poppy, tree poppy) needs little pruning, other than to cut out frost-damaged shoots in mid-spring. It is a subshrubby plant, but in very cold areas is more herbaceous, the foliage dying down in winter.

Rubus (ornamental brambles) are hardy plants, bearing white, pink, red or purple flowers in summer. In late spring cut to ground level all old stems on those species – such as *R. biflorus* – that are grown for their coloured stems. This will encourage the development of fresh ones. With other species cut to ground level a few of the old stems as soon as the flowers have faded.

Spartium junceum (Spanish broom) is a hardy deciduous shrub with rush-like stems that bear golden-yellow, pea-like, fragrant flowers from early to late summer. You should lightly trim young plants several times during summer to encourage bushiness. When they are established, shorten the stems to a third or half of their length in late winter or early summer. Trimming this shrub in autumn is frequently claimed to encourage the development of early flowers.

Symphoricarpos spp. (snowberry) bears little white or pink flowers that are followed by white or bluish-purple berries. In late winter cut out a few of the oldest stems to ground level and remove all crossing or crowded stems.

evergreen shrubs

Evergreen shrubs are clothed in leaves throughout the year, with old leaves continually falling off and new ones being formed to replace them. Once established, these shrubs need no more pruning than to cut out weak, diseased and straggly shoots in spring. Remember that you should never prune evergreen shrubs in winter, as any young shoots that subsequently develop could be blackened and damaged by frosts.

RENOVATING EVERGREENS

The further back into old wood that large, neglected evergreens are cut, the less likely it is that they will develop fresh shoots from their bases and become

Winter damage

In exceptionally cold winters the leaves of evergreen shrubs are often singed and blackened by frost. The edges darken, becoming crisp and brittle. In spring use sharp secateurs to cut out the damaged leaves, together with part of the stem. Cut close to a leaf joint, taking care not leave short stubs, as eventually they decay and encourage the presence of diseases. Never use hand shears to prune large-leaved evergreens; sharp secateurs are much better suited to the job.

Left: Cottage-garden favourite *Lavandula angustifolia* 'Hidcote' (lavender) should be clipped over with shears in late summer to remove dead flowers.

fully clothed with leaves again. Rather than cutting the entire shrub hard back in one season, it is better to spread the pruning over two seasons. In the first spring severely cut back half of the shoots; the following spring prune the remainder. If, after the first pruning, the shrub fails to develop sufficient shoots, cut it back less severely in the second spring.

Evergreen shrubs that respond to being cut hard back include rhododendrons, *Prunus laurocerasus* (cherry laurel), *P. lusitanica* (Portugal laurel), *Buxus sempervirens* (box) and *Olearia* x *haastii* (daisy bush).

TRANSPLANTING EVERGREENS

Occasionally it is necessary to move a large, evergreen shrub from one part of a garden to another, perhaps if the area is being renovated and there are some choice but neglected specimens in it. Just digging up the shrub and moving it makes it difficult for the roots to absorb sufficient moisture to keep the leaves fresh while it is re-establishing itself. In areas where winters are mild, transplanting large evergreens is possible in autumn, when the soil is warm, but in cold areas late spring is a better time to do this.

Before digging up the shrub, shorten long stems and branches by a half to two-thirds. After replanting, mist the foliage and erect a screen to protect the shrub from strong sunshine and cold, drying winds. In spring water the soil and in early summer give it a feed.

TRIMMING HEATHERS

Keep heathers such as *Calluna*, *Erica* and *Daboecia* spp. neat and tidy by trimming them with hand shears. Do not use secateurs for this job because they make it impossible to achieve a smooth, contoured outline. Trim callunas and summer-flowering ericas in spring, lightly clipping off the dead flowers and creating an undulating profile. Take care not to cut into young shoots, however, because these will bear flowers later in the summer.

Trim winter- and spring-flowering *Erica* spp. as soon as their flowers fade. Lightly brush off all the clippings – do not leave them on the plants.

Prune *Daboecia* spp. in late autumn, after flowering finishes. Lightly clip over them with hand shears to remove the old flowerheads. In cold areas, however, you should leave this pruning until spring. At this time, any young shoots that subsequently develop will not be killed by frost.

REJUVENATING SHRUBS

Large, overgrown evergreen shrubs such as *Aucuba japonica* (spotted laurel) can be rejuvenated by cutting all stems back to within 30cm (12in) of the ground in spring. If the shrub is exceptionally large and old, cut the stems at a point 60–90cm (2–3ft) above the ground. Heavy-duty, double-action loppers are usually needed; alternatively, use a curved saw.

Pruning lavender

Lavandula *spp. (lavender) flowers from mid- to late summer and is pruned by lightly trimming over the plants in late summer, using a pair of sharp hand shears. Do not cut into young shoots; just trim off the old flowers. If a plant is straggly, cut the stems hard back in late spring. This encourages the development of young shoots from the plant's base. Lavender hedges are clipped to shape in spring (see pages 78–9).*

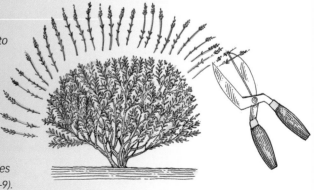

Left: Always remove all-green shoots from variegated shrubs like *Elaeagnus pungens* 'Maculata'.

suggested plants

The following ornamental shrubs provide valuable colour, form and texture throughout the year. Most require little pruning, other than to thin out congested stems or to remove damaged or dead branches.

Abutilon (flowering maple) is a large genus of about 150 species. *A. megapotamicum* (trailing abutilon) is a tender plant that is sometimes semi-evergreen. Grow it against a warm, sunny wall, where it will grow to about 1.8m (6ft). Cut out frost-damaged and straggly shoots in mid-spring. The yellow flowers are borne in summer and autumn. Prune *A. vitifolium* in the same way as *A. megapotamicum*.

Artemisia arborescens is an upright shrub bearing small yellow flowers. Prune by cutting out frosted and congested shoots in early spring.

Aucuba japonica (spotted laurel) needs no regular pruning, but overgrown specimens can be cut back in spring to about 60cm (2ft) above the ground. The edges of leaves sometimes become blackened and singed by frost. In spring, cut back stems bearing damaged leaves.

Berberis spp. need no regular pruning, but if bushes become congested cut back old or exhausted shoots to ground level or healthy main shoots. *B. darwinii* is a hardy evergreen shrub from Chile. Its glossy, dark green, holly-like leaves become hidden during late spring and early summer by pendulous yellow

and orange flowers. These are followed by blue berries. It grows about 2.4m (8ft) high. Prune deciduous berberis in late winter or early spring, when the beauty of their berries is over.

Calluna vulgaris (Scots heather, ling) is a variable or low-growing shrub. Use secateurs to cut back long shoots in early spring. Alternatively, trim over plants with garden shears to remove dead flowers immediately they fade.

Camellia spp. and cultivars are grown for their glossy foliage and beautiful flowers. No regular pruning is needed, but shorten long shoots in mid-spring to produce well-shaped bushes. Plants that are old, with bare stems and bases, can be induced to produce further shoots by being cut back by a third to a half of their height in mid-spring.

Ceanothus (Californian lilac) is a genus containing both evergreen and deciduous shrubs. Prune spring-flowering evergreen species that have been grown as bushes after the flowers fade. Shorten the longest shoots to keep the plant neat and shapely. When evergreen species are grown against walls, cut back strong sideshoots to 3–5cm (1–2in) from the main branches once flowering is over.

Choisya ternata (Mexican orange blossom) produces a wealth of white, sweetly scented, orange-blossom-like flowers mainly in late spring and early summer, then intermittently until autumn. The

evergreen, glossy, dark-green leaves have an orange-like bouquet when crushed. Most gardens can accommodate this slightly tender shrub, which thrives in a warm, wind-sheltered corner and forms a dome about 1.5m (5ft) high. No regular pruning is needed, other than pruning out straggly shoots after the first flush of flowers has faded. Cut out frost-damaged shoots in spring. Rejuvenate old bushes by cutting them hard back in late spring, but this means losing the subsequent summer's flowers.

Daboecia cantabrica (St Dabeoc's heath) needs lime-free soil. Use garden shears to clip off dead flowers in late autumn, after the flowers fade. In cold areas leave pruning until spring.

Daphne spp. need no regular pruning, but occasionally remove straggly shoots in spring. *D. cneorum* (garland flower) is a prostrate, evergreen shrub, to 15cm (6in) high and spreading to 90cm (3ft), with sweetly scented rose-pink flowers in late spring and early summer.

Elaeagnus spp. needs no regular pruning, but in spring cut out misplaced and straggly shoots, and always remove all-green shoots from variegated shrubs. *E. pungens* 'Goldrim' has glossy, dark green leaves. *E. pungens* 'Maculata' has leathery, glossy green leaves splashed with gold. These forms of elaeagnus are ideal for brightening borders in winter and can be planted in full sun or light shade.

Erica (heath, heather) is a genus of more than 700 species. Use garden shears in spring to trim off dead flowers from summer-flowering cultivars. Clip winter- and spring-flowering types as soon as the flowers fade. **Escallonia spp.** need little regular pruning, but occasionally cut back shoots in spring or as soon as the flowers have faded.

Euonymus is a genus of both deciduous and evergreen species. The deciduous ones need no regular pruning, although they are improved by thinning out and shortening shoots in late winter. Evergreen species can be pruned to shape in spring.

Fatsia japonica (syn. *Aralia japonica*; false castor oil plant, Japanese fatsia) needs no pruning unless it becomes necessary to improve the shape. Prune in spring.

Garrya elliptica (silk-tassel bush) needs little pruning when it is grown as a bush. Occasionally cut out a few shoots so that it retains an attractive shape. If it is grown as a wall shrub, cut back long, secondary shoots in spring.

Gaultheria (syn. Pernettya) spp. need no regular pruning but cut back large plants in spring. *G. mucronata* does not need regular pruning, but old plants that become leggy can be severely cut back in late winter or early spring to encourage the development of fresh shoots.

Hebe spp. (shrubby veronica) need no regular pruning, but cut back frost-damaged or straggly shoots in late spring. Also, cut back shrubs that have become leggy during spring.

Helianthemum nummularium (rock rose, sun rose) can be semi-evergreen. Shorten straggly shoots and cut off old flowerheads as soon as the flowers have faded.

Lavandula spp. (lavender) should be clipped over with garden shears in late summer to remove dead flowers. Where plants have been neglected and have become straggly, prune them hard back in spring. This encourages the development of shoots from the shrub's base.

Mahonia spp. need no regular pruning, but *M. aquifolium* (Oregon grape) grown as ground-cover it can be cut hard back each spring.

Pieris spp. need little pruning, but remove dead flowers and, at the same time, cut out straggly shoots. *P. japonica* 'Blush' is ideal for bringing spring colour to gardens, especially if the soil is moist and lime free. It is slow-growing, eventually reaching 1.8m (6ft) high, with flowers that open from rose, when in bud, to pale blue-pink. *P. japonica* 'White Rim' (syn. 'Variegata') has green leaves edged in creamy-white.

Pittosporum is a genus containing about 200 species, which need long, straggly shoots cut out in late spring or early summer.

Pyracantha spp. (firethorn), grown as shrubs in borders, need little pruning, apart from cutting them to shape in late spring or early summer – but avoid cutting off flowers. When they are grown against a wall, shorten long sideshoots in mid-spring, but take care not to cut off too many that would subsequently bear flowers. When wall shrubs become too vigorous, cut them back to old wood in spring, although it means sacrificing the season's flowers.

Rhododendron cvs need no regular pruning, but cut back frost-damaged shoots in spring. If plants are leggy and large, cut them back in mid-spring, if necessary to about 30cm (12in) above the soil.

Rosmarinus officinalis (rosemary) is an aromatic shrub. Cut out dead shoots in spring and shorten the tips of long, straggly shoots. If plants become overcrowded, cut them back in mid-spring.

Santolina chamaecyparissus (cotton lavender) bears yellow flowers in mid- to late summer. Lightly clip off old flowers with hand shears as soon as they fade. Rejuvenate old plants by cutting them hard back in late spring.

Sarcococca spp. (sweet box, Christmas box) bears very fragrant white flowers, followed by bluish-black fruit. When shrubs become crowded, cut out a few of the old stems to ground level after the flowers have faded.

Skimmia spp. need no regular pruning, but shorten long, straggly shoots in spring.

Right: In spring, cut back frost-damaged shoots on rhodendrons.
Far right: Camellias, like this beautiful 'Gloire de Nantes' do not require regular pruning.

2 ROSES

Roses are part of our gardening heritage, and, although they are native only to the northern hemisphere, they are now grown throughout the world. The range of types and cultivars of roses is enormous, partly as a result of the natural promiscuity of many wild roses but also because of the work of hybridizers and rose enthusiasts over the years.

Left: *Rosa* 'Félicité Perpétue'
cloaks a pergola in
sumptuous blooms.
Above: Roses are easier to
prune than many gardeners
realize. Here *Rosa*
'Chinatown' puts on a
beautiful summer display.

Like many other woody, long-lived garden plants, roses are actually shrubs, and to encourage an annual feast of flowers regular pruning is essential. It not only creates magnificent flowers but also ensures the shrub's longevity, especially when it has been planted in poor soil. The quality and size of flowers can also be influenced by the severity with which plants are pruned. The type of pruning needed by hybrid tea roses (now known as large-flowered roses) is quite different from that required by a rambler rose or those used to form hedges.

Regrettably, a mystique about pruning roses has developed, and this has deterred many gardeners from growing them, and yet these floriferous shrubs are some of the most tolerant of all garden shrubs when it comes to bad pruning. If a hybrid tea rose is too severely pruned, only a few stems will develop, but they will bear large blooms. Conversely, if the rose is lightly pruned, many but smaller flowers are produced.

Some roses form bushes, others hug the ground, while a few scale trees or obligingly lean against walls, pergolas or trellises, and if buds are inserted at the tops of tall rootstocks, standard roses can be created. Some roses flower directly on shoots produced from the plant's base, while others develop flowers on young shoots that originate from an existing framework. Each of these roses needs different treatment to encourage the regular creation of flowers.

Pruning bush forms of hybrid teas (large-flowered roses) and floribundas (cluster-flowered roses) has, for many rose lovers, acquired a cult status that has caused unnecessary concern among novice rose growers. We have described here all the traditional methods of pruning, but it is worth remembering that recent trials have involved pruning bush roses with garden shears, just clipping over them. Subsequent flowering has been good, but the long-term effects on the bushes are unknown. Nevertheless, it does underline the point that roses are more resilient and undemanding than many rose growers believe.

Left: If a hybrid tea, like this 'Ena Harkness', is pruned too severely it will develop only a few stems, but they will bear large flowers.
Below right: Established rose bushes are best pruned in early spring.

regular maintenance

Every rosarian has a particular view about the best time to prune roses, but the consensus is that established bushes, and autumn- and winter-planted roses, are best pruned in early spring just when growth is starting but before leaves appear. Bushes that were planted in spring should be pruned immediately after planting. To prevent bushes from being buffeted by winds during winter storms and their roots becoming loosened in the soil, cut back long stems in early winter. If any shoots are infected with disease, burn them.

The correct cut

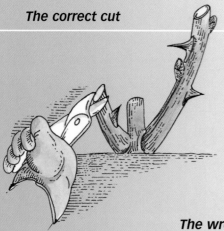

All pruning cuts on roses have traditionally been made individually and with sharp secateurs, and although experiments using hedge clippers are now being investigated, for the present it is best to use secateurs. Do not leave short stubs at the plant's base: they look unsightly and attract diseases. Use sharp secateurs that are large enough to cut the stem cleanly. Make a slightly sloping cut about 6mm (¼in) above an outward-pointing, healthy bud.

The wrong cuts

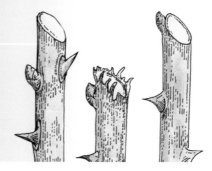

Take care not to make these cuts. The one shown at left is too far above the bud, causing the shoot to die. The one in the centre is the result of using blunt or too small secateurs. The one at right is too close to the bud, leaving it partly unsupported.

MAKING THE RIGHT CUT

Part of the technique of pruning roses is to make clean cuts slightly above outward-pointing buds. This is achieved by using sharp secateurs large enough to tackle the work. Never use small secateurs because they become strained and produce torn, ragged surfaces that do not heal quickly. Make sure you have the right tools and choose tools that will achieve cuts with clean, smooth surfaces. Wear stout gloves to protect your hands.

If you are left-handed, remember that some secateurs have been specially designed for you and make it possible for cuts to be made much more easily than with right-handed types. They also allow left-handed gardeners to see the position of each cut more easily than if they are using a right-handed pair.

Cuts more than 12mm (½in) wide should be painted with a fungicidal wound paint to prevent the entry of diseases and to give protection from damp and frost.

bush roses

Pruning hybrid tea roses (large-flowered roses) and floribunda roses (cluster-flowered roses) has acquired an unnecessary mystique, yet basically it is a logical process and entirely influenced by the nature of these plants. Both types of rose are deciduous shrubs that produce their best flowers on new shoots developed earlier in the year. The size and number of new shoots that bush roses develop each year is dictated by the degree of severity with which they are pruned. Pruning is also influenced by the type of soil, whether exhibition blooms are desired and whether the plants are young. This may appear complicated, but if a step-by-step approach is adopted, it is quite straightforward. Usually, after a couple of years of pruning bush roses, it becomes clear what degree of severity is required for the roses in your garden.

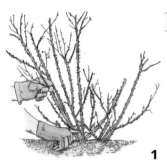

1

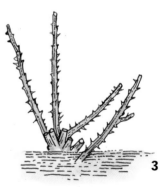

3

PREPARATORY PRUNING

Whether you are pruning hybrid tea or floribunda bush roses, the initial task is the same.

1 Cut out dead wood directly at the shrub's base. Also, remove shoots that have been damaged by wind blowing them against each other, and cut out those infected by disease. If the cut surface is brown, the stem is infected and a lower cut is needed where the wood is white. Never leave damaged shoots.

2 Cut out thin, weak and spindly shoots right to their bases. Make sure that the centre of the shrub is open and that air can circulate throughout the bush. This helps shoots to ripen, enabling them to resist the entry of disease.

3 The shoots that remain should be strong, healthy and well spaced. The severity of pruning during this last stage is influenced by several factors, such as whether the rose is newly planted, the type of soil and whether the rose is a hybrid tea or floribunda. The next stage is to prune them either 'hard', 'moderately' or 'lightly', as illustrated opposite.

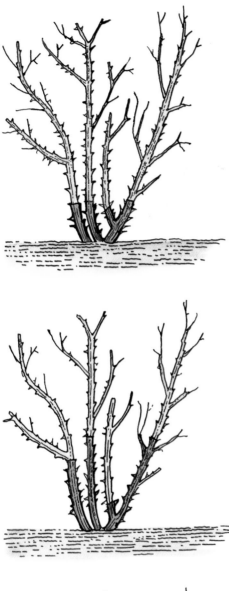

HARD PRUNING

In hard pruning, sometimes called low pruning, stems are cut back to three or four buds above the plant's base. This leaves short stems 13–15cm (5–6in) long. This approach is ideal for newly planted hybrid tea and floribunda roses because it encourages strong shoots to develop from the base. It is not suitable for most established bush roses, although weak-growing hybrid teas are frequently hard pruned, and it is often used to rejuvenate neglected hybrid teas, but not established floribundas.

MODERATE PRUNING

In moderate, or medium, pruning, stems are cut back by about a half their length, although weak ones need more severe treatment. This approach is ideal for most hybrid tea and floribunda roses, especially those growing in ordinary soil. If, after a few years, hybrid tea types become too high and leggy, prune hard in one season.

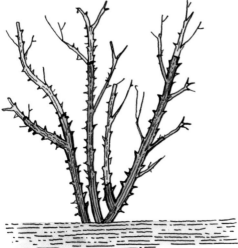

LIGHT PRUNING

In light pruning, which is sometimes known as high or long pruning, the top third of all shoots is removed. The approach is frequently used on vigorous hybrid tea roses, because it does not encourage the further growth of strong shoots, and restricts the plant's height. It is the ideal method for all bush roses growing in sandy soils, where the fertility is low and insufficient to provide the vigorous growth encouraged by hard pruning.

Left: This hedge of *Rosa gallica* var. *officinalis* (apothecary's rose) is an eye-catching feature in the summer garden.

PRUNING GROUP 1 ROSES

When you are planting these roses, cut off coarse and weak roots. Also, shorten damaged and unripe shoots. In the first and second years, cut out a few old shoots in winter.

species & shrub roses

Species and shrub roses are increasingly capturing the attention of rose specialists as well as people new to gardening. These are roses with a more natural appearance than modern types, such as hybrid teas and floribundas, and they are ideal for planting in shrub or mixed borders where informality is desired. They include many that are native to various parts of the northern hemisphere – Europe, North America and Asia – as well as natural and cultivated crosses between two species.

Because many of these roses have been growing for thousands of years without interference from gardeners, it is often suggested that they should be left alone to follow their own habits and to grow naturally. This may suit some of them, but it is certainly not true for all. By careful pruning, it is possible to prevent them from becoming congested with unwanted growth and thereby to give them a longer and more floriferous lifespan.

It may be thought that all species and shrub roses have the same character and need similar pruning techniques, but nothing could be further from the truth. For the convenience of gardeners, however, it is possible to simplify the pruning of these roses by categorizing them into three groups, although there are many types that do not fit into this classification.

Group 1 roses

Roses in this group include:
- *Species roses (but not climbers) and their close hybrids*
- Rosa rugosa *(Japanese rose, ramanas rose) and hybrids*
- *R. pimpinellifolia (burnet rose, Scotch rose) and hybrids*
- *R. gallica var. officinalis (apothecary's rose)*
- *Hybrid musks*

1 In late winter or early spring of the second year, completely cut off shoots that have developed from the plant's base and are badly positioned. Also, cut back the tips of vigorous shoots.

2 In the subsequent summer, the plant will produce flowers on shoots borne on old wood. At the same time, strong, new shoots will develop directly from the shrub's base.

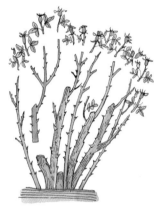

3 In early autumn of the same year, after the flowers have faded, cut out thin and weak growths, as well as those that may be damaged or diseased. Also, cut back the tip of each shoot.

4 In the third and subsequent years, regular pruning is essential. In late winter or early spring cut back lateral shoots. Also, cut out at their bases one or two old shoots.

5 In mid- and late summer of the same year, the shrub will bear flowers on lateral shoots that have developed on the old shoots. In the same summer fresh shoots will grow from the shrub's base.

6 In early autumn, cut back the tips of shoots to encourage the development of laterals that will bear flowers in the following year. Cut out thin and weak shoots and totally remove old ones.

PRUNING GROUP 2 ROSES

When you are planting roses in this group cut off damaged and weak roots and lightly cut back the tips of diseased and thin shoots.

2 From mid- to late summer of the second year, flowers will be borne on lateral shoots that were cut back earlier. In this period new shoots will be growing from the shrub's base. Cut off the flowers as they fade.

1 In late winter or early spring of the second year, cut back by about a third all those shoots that earlier developed from the shrub's base. In addition, cut back to two or three eyes all laterals that developed on flowered shoots.

3 Slightly later, from early to late autumn of the second year, cut back shoots that are extra long. By doing this, the risk of the shrub being damaged or roots loosened by strong wind in late autumn and winter is reduced.

Group 2 roses

Roses in this group include roses that flower chiefly on short lateral shoots as well as sub-laterals originating from two-year-old, or older, wood, including:
● Rosa x alba *and hybrids*
● R. centifolia *and hybrids*
● *Moss roses*
● *Most damask roses*
● *Modern shrub roses that have one main flush of bloom in midsummer*

4 In late winter and early spring of the third and subsequent years, cut back by a third new shoots that developed from ground level. Also cut back laterals on flowered shoots to two or three eyes. Then cut out a few old shoots at the base.

Right: Follow the steps for Group 2 roses to prune *Rosa* 'Centifolia Variegata'.

5 From mid- to late summer of the same year, the bush will bear flowers on lateral shoots that were cut back earlier. The cycle of fresh shoots growing each year and later developing sideshoots that will bear flowers is repeated the following season.

6 Later in the season, from early to late autumn, cut off the ends of stems that are extra-long. This reduces the area of stems and helps to prevent the shrub's roots being disturbed when shoots are blown by strong winds in late autumn and winter.

Group 3 roses

Species and shrub roses in this group include most China and Bourbon roses and many modern shrub types. Although they have a similar nature to those detailed in group 2, they differ in that they flower recurrently throughout summer and into autumn both on the current season's shoots and on laterals and sub-laterals that develop from both two-year and older shoots. Because many of the flowers are borne on laterals on old wood, these plants soon become congested if pruning is neglected. Therefore, regularly remove dead flowers and thin out twiggy clusters in summer. In addition, encourage the development of fresh shoots from ground level by cutting out old ones in winter. At the same time cut out all diseased shoots.

Left: Rosa pimpinellifolia 'Dunwich Rose' has large white flowers which are in crisp contrast to the foliage.
Right above: The rich crimson flowers of the gallica rose 'Tuscany Superb' fade to light purple.
Right below: 'Buff Beauty' is treasured for its soft apricot blooms and sturdy growth.

species and shrub roses:
group 1

Roses within this pruning group (see pages 34–5) include the Burnet rose, hybrid musks, *Rosa rugosa* and *Rosa gallica*. These roses have a dense, bushy nature, with flowers mainly on short lateral and sub-lateral shoots arising from two-year-old and older wood.

BURNET ROSE

The Burnet rose, *Rosa pimpinelli-folia* (syn. *R. spinosissima),* is also occasionally called the Scotch rose because of the many hybrids and varieties that were created and popularized by Scottish nurserymen as early as the beginning of the nineteenth century. *R. pimpinellifolia* is rarely more than 1.2m (4ft) high, with a suckering habit, and it forms a thicket of erect, slender stems that bear small, white, creamy-white or pale pink flowers in late spring and early summer.

Popular varieties include *R. pimpinellifolia* 'Grandiflora' (syn. *R. p.* 'Altaica'), which has large, single, white flowers. The double white form, which grows to 60–90cm (2–3ft), has an exquisite charm, with lily-of-the-valley-scented, double, globular, white flowers. *R. pimpinellifolia* 'William III' has semi-double flowers, with purplish-crimson flowers that fade to lilac-pink.

Known in Scotland as Prince Charlie's rose, *R. x harisonii* 'Williams' Double Yellow' is slightly taller than the species and often said to be related to *R. foetida* (the Austrian briar). It has double, heavily scented, deep yellow blooms. In some earlier catalogues it was listed as 'Double Yellow'. *R. x harisonii* 'Lutea Maxima' is a superb single yellow rose, with both the Austrian briar and the Burnet rose among its ancestors.

HYBRID MUSKS

These roses have a graceful, refined nature with delicately coloured flowers, which are borne in large trusses. Varieties in this group include 'Ballerina', which has hydrangea-like heads of single, blossom-pink flowers; 'Buff Beauty', which grows to about 1.5m (5ft) across and high, is well known for its sturdy growth, handsome foliage and large trusses of warm apricot-yellow flowers; 'Cornelia', which has rosette-shaped, coppery-apricot flowers, which fade to coppery-pink; 'Felicia' is a strong-growing rose with silvery-pink flowers that deepen towards their centre; and 'Prosperity' has scented, large trusses of ivory-white, semi-double flowers.

RUGOSA ROSES

Rosa rugosa is known as the hedgehog rose, Japanese rose or ramanas rose. 'Ramanas' was said to be the Japanese name for this rose, but was mistaken for 'hamanas', itself a corruption of 'hama-nashi' ('shore-pear'). It has spawned many hardy, strong-growing and vibrantly coloured varieties. They all are superb, but those of special merit include 'Agnes', which has scented, rich yellow and amber flowers; 'Blanche Double de Coubert' has pure white, semi-double flowers; 'Fru Dagmar Hastrup' has single, pink flowers delicately veined and with cream stamens; 'Lady Curzon' has single, pink flowers; 'Mrs Anthony Waterer' has richly fragrant crimson flowers; 'Roseraie de l'Haÿ', a dense and vigorous plant to 1.8–2.1m (6–7ft), has strongly scented flowers, with large, wine-purple buds that open to a glorious crimson-purple; 'Sarah van Fleet' has slightly cupped, semi-double, mallow-pink flowers with cream stamens; 'Scabrosa' has large, single, crimson flowers tinged with violet; and 'Snowdon', which is a more recent introduction, with fully double, rosette-like, pure white blooms.

GALLICA ROSES

R. gallica var. *officinalis*, which is also known as the Provins rose, the apothecary's rose and the red rose of Lancaster, is a suckering shrub with erect, bristly stems that has given rise to many hybrids. Well-known forms include: 'Belle de Crécy', which has rich cerise-pink flowers that slowly turn to soft violet; 'Camaïeux', with white flowers, which are striped and splashed with crimson; 'Charles de Mills', which is a strongly growing rose to about 1.5m (5ft) high and 1.2m (4ft) across, with

large, full-petalled, rich crimson flowers, turning purple as they age; *R.* x *francofurtana* (syn. 'Empress Josephine'), which has large, clear pink flowers, veined in deep pink; and 'Tuscany Superb', which has deep crimson flowers, fading to light purple.

Left: 'Frülingsmorgen' is a modern shrub rose. The stunning flowers are pink with primrose yellow centres.
Right above: The heady scent and pretty pink colour of the Alba rose 'Königin von Dänemark' make it worthy of any garden.
Right below: 'William Lobb' (syn. 'Duchess d'Istrie') is a moss rose, popular for its double, crimson flowers.

species and shrub roses:
group 2

Roses in pruning group 2 (see pages 38–9) include several of the so-called old roses, together with those modern shrub roses which have a main flush of flowers in midsummer but are not repeat-flowering.

OLD ROSES

This group includes the Albas, among which are 'Alba Maxima' (often known as the Jacobite rose or great white rose), which has double, creamy-white flowers that are initially blush pink; 'Céleste', which has semi-double, sweetly scented and shell pink flowers; 'Félicité Parmentier', which has slightly ball-shaped, fresh pink flowers, creamy at the edges; and 'Königin von Dänemark' (syn. 'Queen of Denmark'), which has strongly scented, large, quartered blooms of soft, glowing pink, with attractive, grey-green leaves.

CENTIFOLIAS

Also known as Provence or cabbage roses, because they usually have large and globular, scented blooms, the centifolia roses include *R*. x *centifolia* 'Cristata' (syn. 'Chapeau de Napoléon' and often known as the crested moss rose), which has richly fragrant, pure pink flowers; 'Fantin-Latour', with cupped, blush pink flowers, which deepen to shell pink at their centre and curl backwards as they open; 'Robert le Diable', which has flowers that are purple-shaded with slate-grey and splashed with scarlet and cerise; and 'Tour de Malakoff', which has large, open blooms, at first magenta-purple, later violet and then lavender and grey.

MOSS ROSES

The moss roses are closely related to the centifolias, but they have developed green moss-like growths on their sepals, the outer part of the flower. Popular in Victorian times, they are now represented by varieties such as 'Comtesse de Murinais', which has full-petalled,

blush pink flowers, deepening to salmon pink; 'Général Kléber', which has large, flat and quartered, soft mauve-pink flowers; 'Gloire des Mousseuses', which has fragrant, clear pink blooms; 'Louis Gimard', which has large, globular, cupped, light crimson flowers with lilac tones; 'René d'Anjou', which has fragrant, soft pink flowers; and 'William Lobb' (syn. 'Duchesse d'Istrie'), which has dark crimson, richly scented flowers that fade to violet-grey

DAMASK ROSES

This group is said to have been brought from the Middle East by crusaders. Most of them are fragrant. Varieties to consider include 'Celsiana', which has semi-double, soft pink blooms with golden stamens; 'La Ville de Bruxelles', which has fully double, rich pink, very fragrant flowers; 'Madame Hardy', which is a superb rose, with initially cupped, white flowers; and 'Marie Louise', which has very large and intense pink flowers.

MODERN SHRUB ROSES

Modern shrub roses have a main display in midsummer, and there is no repeat flowering. Recommended varieties include 'Cerise Bouquet', which has semi-double, cerise-pink flowers; 'Frühlingsgold', which has pale yellow flowers; 'Frühlings-morgen', which has pink flowers; and 'Scharlachglut' (syn. 'Scarlet Fire'), which has scarlet flowers.

Left: The scented, purple-pink flowers of *Rosa* 'Madame Isaac Pereire' are produced abundantly all through summer.
Right above: 'Reine des Violettes' is a spreading hybrid perpetual with grey-tinged foliage and fragrant flowers, in shades of violet and purple.
Right below: The dramatic flowers of *Rosa* x *odorata* 'Mutabilis' change from coppery yellow to pink and then to copper-crimson.

species and shrub roses:
group 3

Roses within this pruning group (see pages 34–5) include most of the China types, some modern shrub roses, many Bourbons and most hybrid perpetuals. They develop flowers on lateral and sub-lateral shoots.

CHINA ROSES
China roses are usually slightly tender and are best planted in frost-free positions. This group includes 'Hermosa', which has fragrant, globular, small pink flowers; *R.* x *odorata* 'Mutabilis', which has pointed, flame-coloured buds that open to reveal coppery-yellow, single flowers, changing to pink and, finally, coppery-crimson; *R.* x *odorata* 'Pallida' (the old blush China rose), which develops graceful clusters of pale pink flowers through most of summer and well into autumn; and 'Sophie's Perpetual', which bears sprays of small, deep pink flowers.

BOURBON ROSES
These roses are the result of crossing China roses with Portland types. They usually have a rich fragrance, and varieties in this group include 'Madame Isaac Pereire', which is a vigorous rose, with large madder-crimson flowers and a rich fragrance; 'Zéphirine Drouhin', a Bourbon climber, which has a glorious fragrance, thornless stems and bright, carmine-pink, semi-double flowers; and 'Madame Ernest Calvat', which bears double, pale to mid-pink, fragrant flowers.

HYBRID PERPETUALS
These roses were very popular in Victorian and Edwardian times, and robust forms of them can be put into pruning group 3. Examples include 'Baron Girod de l'Ain', which has dark crimson flowers that are cup-shaped at first but later opening wide; 'Baronne Prévost', which has pink flowers; 'Gloire de Ducher', which has large, deep crimson, fragrant flowers that slowly become purple; and 'Reine des Violettes', which has flowers in shades of violet and purple and greyish foliage.

Left: Standard roses like this *Rosa* 'Bonica' can act as focal points to create added interest and height in the garden.

standard roses

Standard roses are especially useful in gardens. They can be planted as centrepieces and focal points as well as dotted among bush types to create height in borders. They are ideal for formal situations.

Standard roses are usually formed by budding hybrid tea (large-flowered bush) and floribunda (cluster-flowered bush) roses on to the tops of rootstocks that form the strong, upright stems. Full standards have stems 1.2–1.5m (4–5ft) high; half-standards have stems about 90cm (3ft) high. Half-standards are not as popular as they were in earlier years. Although most standards are formed from hybrid tea and floribunda varieties, some English roses, old roses and shrub types are used. With all these roses, strong stakes and ties are essential to prevent the stem from bending under the weight of flowers and leaves, especially in windy areas or when the foliage is wet and the plants are in full bloom.

SINGLE OR DOUBLE BUDDED?

The best and most easily managed standard roses have two buds inserted into the top of the rootstock. This helps to ensure that from all angles the standard's head is evenly shaped and attractive. One bud may grow more vigorously than the other. If this happens, pruning the weaker shoot more severely than the other one will correct the imbalance.

When only one bud has been used – and it is best not to buy such a plant – it is essential initially to cut back the shoot that develops from it to three or four eyes so that a strong framework with evenly spaced shoots is created. If this is neglected, the head will never be attractive and evenly balanced. Unbalanced heads are, moreover, more likely to be damaged by strong winds than those with an even spread of shoots.

PATIO AND MINIATURE STANDARDS

These roses are becoming increasingly popular, and they are ideal for growing in tubs as well as around patios. They are superb in small gardens. Patio standards have stems about 75cm (2ft 6in) high, and they form dense, rounded heads with masses of flowers in much of summer and into autumn. There are many varieties to consider, including 'Cider Cup' (peach), 'Red Rascal' (red) and 'Sweet Magic' (orange). Miniature standards have stems only 50cm (20in) high. Varieties to consider include 'Orange Sunblaze' (scarlet), 'Pink Sunblaze' (pink) and 'Top Marks' (bright orange-red).

PRUNING STANDARD ROSES

1 In the late winter or early spring after being planted, cut back strong stems on hybrid tea varieties to three to four eyes of their bases. With floribundas, cut stems to six to eight eyes.

2 In the following autumn or early winter, cut off the flowerheads and completely remove soft, unripe and thin shoots. This reduces the risk of wind damaging the standard's head in early winter.

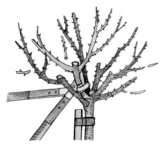

3 In late winter and early spring of the following year, the first task is to cut out dead, weak and diseased shoots. Also cut out crossing shoots.

4 Cut new shoots on hybrid teas to three to five eyes, and laterals to two to four. With floribundas, cut new shoots to six to eight eyes, and laterals to three to six eyes.

Weeping standards

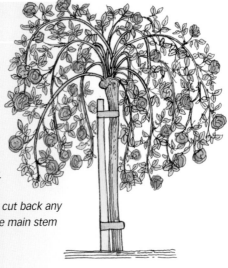

These are a popular form of standard rose and have a cascading, weeping appearance. They are mainly produced by budding rambler varieties on 1.2–1.8m (4–6ft) tall stems of Rosa rugosa.

Pruning is quite simple. In late summer or early autumn, completely cut out two-year-old shoots that have flowers. This will leave young shoots that developed earlier in summer to produce flowers in the following year.

If there are insufficient young stems to replace the old ones that are cut out, leave a few of these older ones and cut back any lateral shoots on them to two or three eyes. Make sure the main stem is secured to a stake.

Left: 'New Dawn' is a vigorous, hardy rose, ideal for growing up a pillar.

pillar roses

Growing climbing roses on poles 2.4–3m (8–10ft) high is an ideal way to create beacons of colour in gardens, especially if it is not possible to grow them against walls or fences. Suitable varieties have an upright nature, with stems about 3m (10ft) high.

PRUNING PILLAR ROSES

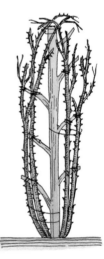

1 In the first summer after being planted, pillar roses develop long stems. Train these in an upright manner and secure them to a brick pillar or a rustic pole, preferably one where a few short branches have been left to create support for stems. They also help to keep the plant's centre open, with a lax appearance.

Roses to grow on pillars

- 'Aloha' (pink)
- 'Bantry Bay' (pink)
- 'Dortmund' (red, with a white eye)
- 'Galway Bay' (pink)
- 'Golden Showers' (golden-yellow),
- 'New Dawn' (silvery-pink)
- 'Pink Perpétué' (pink with a carmine reverse)
- 'White Cockade' (white).

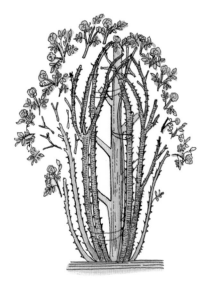

2 In the following summer, the plant bears flowers on small, lateral shoots that have grown on the long stems that developed in the previous year. In addition, in summer, fresh, long shoots develop from the plant's base. Cut off all flowers as they fade to keep the plant tidy, removing the complete flower truss.

3 In late autumn or early winter of the same year, cut back all lateral shoots that developed flowers. Prune back some of the young shoots produced in the year, attempting to retain a symmetrical outline. Make sure that they are spread evenly around the plant and not all clustered on the sunny side.

4 Also in late autumn or early winter of the same year, cut out weak shoots that have developed from the plant's base. In addition, remove diseased and dead wood and totally cut out a few of the very old shoots. The cycle of cutting out old stems and training in new ones must be repeated each year. If this is neglected, the plant will become a mass of tangled shoots that produce very few flowers.

5 In the following and subsequent years, lateral shoots on the previous year's growth will bear flowers in summer. Cut these off as they fade. In late autumn or early winter of the same year, cut out all laterals that produced flowers. Totally sever old wood and completely remove a few of the old stems. Pillar roses are usually very easy to prune, as all the shoots are easy to reach.

rambling & climbing roses

Although climbers and ramblers have a leaning nature and many happily scale trees or lean against walls, they each have a distinct character. Ramblers develop numerous small flowers that are held in large bunches that appear in early and midsummer. They flower only once a year and the plant then devotes its energies to producing strong canes that will bear flowers in the following season. Climbers have larger flowers, often similar to other garden roses, and they are borne singly or in small groups. Some climbers also have the ability to produce further flowers after their first period in bloom. Although these distinctions are clear in theory, they are complicated by the wide range of varieties and varied derivations of both ramblers and climbers. Ramblers are discussed here; climbing roses are described on pages 50–1. Some climbers, including 'Golden Showers', 'Pink Perpétué' and 'White Cockade', are also trained as pillar roses, and these are described on pages 46–7.

Rambling roses

There are three main types:
- *Multiflora hybrids have large bunches of small flowers, with stiff growth (pruning group 2)*
- *Sempervirens hybrids are graceful ramblers, with long, strong growth and sprays of small flowers; they are (pruning group 1)*
- *Wichuraiana hybrids have long, graceful growths and quite large flowers borne in elegant sprays, and they develop long, flexible shoots from their bases (pruning group 1); some rose experts suggest they can be left with little pruning, but they then eventually form thickets*

PRUNING GROUP 1 RAMBLERS

1 From late autumn to early spring, when a rambler is bought from a nursery, cut back coarse, unevenly long roots. The rose will also probably have three or four stems, each up to 1.2m (4ft) long. Cut these back to 23–38cm (9–15in) long. Then plant it firmly in good, well-drained soil.

2 In spring, young shoots will develop from buds at the top of each stem. These will form the initial flowering stems and framework, although the aim must eventually be to encourage fresh shoots to develop from the plant's base each year.

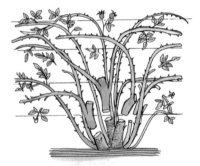

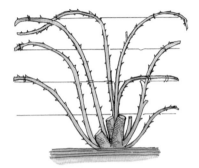

3 In late summer or autumn of the following year (as well as all subsequent ones), cut out flowered shoots to their bases, leaving, tying in and spacing out on supports all strong shoots that developed earlier that season. Take care not to damage these shoots by tying them too tightly.

4 At the same time, cut back all shoots that are growing from these main ones to within two or three eyes of their base. Rejuvenate neglected ramblers by cutting all shoots back. Although this means losing the following season's flowers, it is the best way to restore regular flowering.

Left: Rosa 'Albertine' has scented, double flowers.
Left above: Here *Rosa* 'Veilchenblau' scrambles through a tree. The foliage of tree is an elegant foil for the violet roses.

Pruning group 2 ramblers

The pruning of these plants is the same in the first year as for those in group 1, which they closely resemble, although they develop fewer shoots from their bases. Prune them immediately after the flowers fade, completely cutting out old shoots and training in new ones. If no basal shoots are present, cut the old stems to within 38cm (15in) of the bases. Also, cut back old shoots higher up on the plant to vigorous sideshoots and cut short lateral shoots back to two or three eyes above their point of origin.

PRUNING GROUP 3 CLIMBERS

The pruning and training schedule described should be repeated every year. Completely cut out old and exhausted stems to within a few inches of the climber's base to encourage fresh, strong growths to develop.

Above: 'Madame Grégoire Staechelin' is a vigorous climber with large clusters of pink blooms.
Below: 'Golden Showers' is a modern climber which flowers profusely all summer.

Climbing roses

The following roses are classified as pruning group 3:
- *Noisette roses are an old group, with small, rosette-type flowers; they need a warm, frost-free position*
- *Climbing tea roses are similar to the Noisettes, but with more of a hybrid tea appearance*
- *Climbing hybrid teas have a hybrid tea nature and are usually sports (natural mutations) of hybrid teas*
- *Climbing Bourbons are characterized by their old rose type flowers; like most other climbers, they are repeat-flowering*
- *Modern climbers are a relatively new group with a repeat-flowering nature, with flowers resembling those of hybrid teas*

1 In the dormant season, when a young climber is bought from a nursery, cut back coarse and uneven roots. In addition, cut out weak shoots at the bases and lightly cut back the tips of unripe and damaged shoots. Then, plant it firmly and space out and loosely tie in the stems to create a permanent framework.

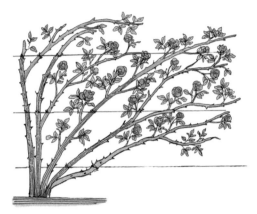

2 In mid- and late summer of the following season, continue to tie in new shoots that develop from the existing framework, as well as those that grow from ground level. Also, train in strong shoots that develop from the main framework. The formation of this framework distinguishes climbers from ramblers, which each season replace stems that are cut out with fresh shoots from ground level. In the case of climbers, a permanent framework is created. A few flowers will appear at the ends of new shoots. As soon as the flowers fade, cut them off. Do not be disappointed if only a few flowers appear; it is more important to build up the plant's framework.

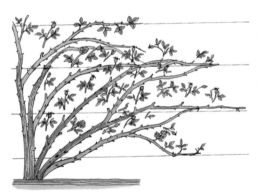

3 Between mid-autumn of the same year and early spring of the following year, cut back all lateral shoots that have borne flowers to within three or four eyes of their points of origin. In addition, cut out weak and diseased shoots and tie in leading shoots to the framework. Thin and weak shoots arising from the climber's base should also be cut out. If pruning is left until early spring, also cut out frost-damaged shoots, especially from slightly tender varieties which have been given a too cold or wind-exposed position. Loose shoots that repeatedly flap against supports may also be damaged: check all loose shoots and cut them out as necessary.

4 In the following mid- and late summer, flowers are borne on the tips of new growths as well as on lateral shoots. When the flowers fade, cut them off. Also tie in new shoots as they grow. Later in the same season, from mid-autumn to early spring, cut back all lateral shoots that have borne flowers to three or four eyes of their point of origin. At the same time, cut out weak and diseased shoots and tie in to a supporting framework of leading shoots.

3 CLIMBING PLANTS

Most gardens have space for climbing plants.
Walls and fences can be brightened, while
pergolas and rustic poles offer further decorative
opportunities. Apart from glorious arrays of
flowers, many climbers produce colourful leaves
and berries in a feast of rich autumn hues.

Deciduous climbers that create the best display of autumnal colour include the well-known *Parthenocissus tricuspidata* (Boston ivy) and *P. quinquefolia* (Virginia creeper). As well as being a feature in their own right, evergreen climbers also create backgrounds for other garden plants. A few climbers are vigorous enough to grow up through trees, where they can brighten what may be an old and unattractive feature. In addition to giving support for plants, some walls provide sheltered, sun-saturated places for shrubs with a leaning nature that are too tender to be planted in a border. There are also wall shrubs such as pyracantha that survive on exposed, cold walls in extremely cold temperate regions.

The nature of climbing plants varies widely. Some are able to cling to brickwork with great ease, whatever the height. Others are leaners and need a wall or trellis to support them and to which they can be tied. Then there are stems with thorns that hook over supports, either trellises or trees, and scramble their way upwards. Yet other climbers have tendrils that loop around their hosts.

These different ways of climbing influence the supports and type of pruning needed. For instance, *Hedera* spp. (ivy) tenaciously cling to walls and the only pruning necessary is to thin them out and to restrain their spread. Conversely, *Jasminum nudiflorum* (winter-flowering jasmine) is a leaner and as well as having old, flowered stems removed also needs to have the new ones loosely tied to a supporting framework.

The nature of a climber influences where it is planted, what support it is given and the method of pruning. Understanding a climber's character is fundamental to growing it to perfection, and the features of the climbers mentioned in this section are summarized on pages 55–5. Most climbers have a permanent or yearly renewable framework

Left: Hedera canariensis 'Variegata', here combined with *Rosa* 'Golden Showers,' is a popular evergreen climber.
Above: Passiflora caerulea (passion flower) uses tendrils to cling to its support.

of stems, and these 'woody' types are featured here. Others have a herbaceous nature and need only their old stems to be severed and removed at the end of the growing season. There are, of course, annual climbers, but as these do not require pruning – only support and initial guidance – they are not included here.

In addition to climbers, many shrubs are ideal for growing against walls; a few of these shrubs are evergreen and create a permanent array of leaves, while others are deciduous and therefore are barren of colour in winter, a reflection of their less hardy nature.

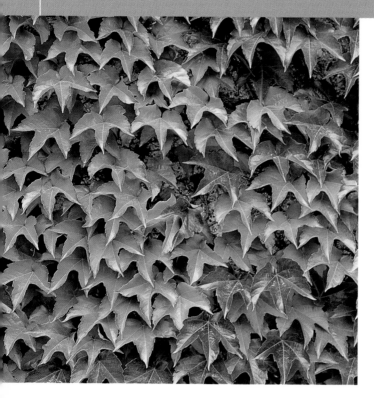

Left: *Parthenocissus tricuspidata* (Boston ivy) is a deciduous, self-supporting climber.
Right above: *Hedera helix* 'Buttercup', like all ivies, is self-clinging.
Right below: The leaves of the twining climber *Actinidia kolomikta* are an unusual combination of green, creamy-white and pink.

climbing habits

Most woody, perennial climbers live for 15 or more years, some a great deal longer. For some of these plants, longevity depends on regular pruning and the cutting out of old, congested and dead stems to encourage the development of fresh shoots. Part of the success in growing climbers is in providing them with suitable places to scale or surfaces to which they can cling. It is no good, for example, expecting a clematis to scale a wall without the provision of wires or a trellis; in such a position, self-clinging climbers, such as *Hedera* spp. (ivy), *Parthenocissus quinquefolia* (Virginia creeper) and *P. henryana* (Chinese Virginia creeper), are better.

Before selecting a climber it is essential to find out about its nature and if a supporting framework is required. It may be thought that all climbers that are self-clinging and scale walls never need pruning, and that all of those that use tendrils to help them climb are pruned in the same way. Unfortunately, this is not so.

HOW THEY CLIMB

Climbers are a disparate group, a conglomeration of plants from many parts of the world. Some of them are totally hardy in temperate regions, others are native to warmer areas and need hospitable homes against a warm, wind-sheltered wall. They can be arranged into four groups.

The first of these groups encompasses climbers with no visible means of support, and they are considered to be nature's leaners. Good examples of these are *Abutilon megapotamicum* (trailing abutilon), *Jasminum nudiflorum* (winter-flowering jasmine), *Solanum crispum* (Chilean potato tree) and, of course, roses, although many of these have large thorns that assist stems to latch on to supports. There are other leaners, including members of the bramble family.

Climbers in the second group are entirely self-supporting; they use adhesive discs or aerial roots to cling to surfaces. *Hedera* spp. (ivy), *Hydrangea anomala* subsp. *petiolaris* (climbing hydrangea), *Parthenocissus henryana* and *P. quinquefolia* are examples of self-supporting types. The only pruning that is necessary with these climbers is to restrain them and occasionally to cut out dead shoots.

The third group is formed of climbers that use tendrils to cling to their hosts or supports. All shrubby clematis are in this group, together with *Passiflora caerulea* (passion flower) and the vines in the grape vine family, including *Vitis coignetiae* (Japanese crimson glory vine).

The fourth group of climbers includes those that twine around their hosts, supporting themselves and often creating a mass of stems. These include *Actinidia kolomikta*, *Jasminum officinale* (common jasmine), *Lonicera periclymenum* (common honeysuckle), wisteria and *Fallopia baldschuania* (Russian vine), which is suitable only for the very largest of gardens and the sturdiest of supports.

HOUSE SECURITY

Few gardeners consider the security implications when they plant climbers against house walls. At one time, the only use of a climber – apart from its aesthetic qualities – was for juvenile pranksters to escape from bedrooms. Nowadays, unfortunately, strong-stemmed climbers, together with a wooden trellis, offer rapid access to the outside of an upstairs window when houses are not constantly attended.

Not all climbers, however, create good and secure footholds: small-leaved ivies such as *Hedera helix* 'Oro di Bogliasco' (syn. *H. helix* 'Goldheart') will not give sufficient support, nor will large-leaved types like *H. colchica* (Persian ivy) or *H. canariensis* 'Gloire de Marengo' (syn. *H. canariensis* 'Variegata'; Canary island ivy), unless they are many years old and have become tangled. The large-flowered clematis hybrids and the species clematis are not

security risks either. Old, long-established wisterias, with thickened bases and well-established stems, present the biggest security risk, as do newly installed trellises that, if well secured to walls, are just like ladders. Old climbing roses may appear to offer easy access, but their thorn-clad stems do not make hospitable hand- and foot-

holds. In addition, their stems are whippy and not supportive.

If you have worries about house security, grow climbers only on pergolas, garden walls and free-standing trellises. Also, climbers such as roses can be encouraged to climb tall trees, while species clematis and large-leaved ivies can be used to clothe tree trunks.

Left: Left unpruned, honeysuckle will continue to flower but will tend to develop into a mass of thin, tangled stems that bear foliage and flowers only at the tops of the shoots. *Right*: *Lonicera periclymenum* 'Belgica' (early Dutch honeysuckle) is an undemanding plant to grow.

renovating climbers

The word 'climbers' covers plants with a wide range of growing and flowering habits. Many need yearly pruning to encourage the development of flowers, while some can continue in an unpruned state until they reach a stage when renovation is essential. Left to nature, many climbers rely on old and woody shoots to create support for new shoots, but gardeners are less tolerant of old, unproductive shoots and, where possible, like to remove them and provide climbers with artificial support.

When you are constructing supports, make sure that stems can pass around both sides of vertical and horizontal rails. With pergolas and rustic poles this is always possible, but if a wooden trellis is secured to a wall it is essential that at least 2–3cm (1in) – and preferably 3.5cm (1½in) – is allowed between the framework and wall.

RENOVATING A CLIMBER

Eventually – and especially if they are neglected over several years – many climbers develop a tangled web of old wood. Slowly, the climber's ability to flower is diminished and it becomes full of congested, old, unflowering shoots. Renovating a climber is best performed in spring.

1 Cut out as much of the old, congested growth as possible. Usually it is a matter of repeatedly snipping out small pieces of entangled shoots.

2 Use sharp secateurs or knife to cut out old, dead, twiggy shoots back to a healthy stem.

Renovating honeysuckle

Honeysuckle evokes thoughts of canopies and arbours drenched in fragrant flowers. Sadly, in many ways some honeysuckles – including Lonicera japonica (Japanese honeysuckle), L. periclymenum 'Belgica' (early Dutch honeysuckle) and L. periclymenum 'Serotina' (late Dutch honeysuckle) – are too undemanding for their own good and will continue to flower for many years without having to be pruned. In time, however, the weight of their leaves and stems can often break their supports.

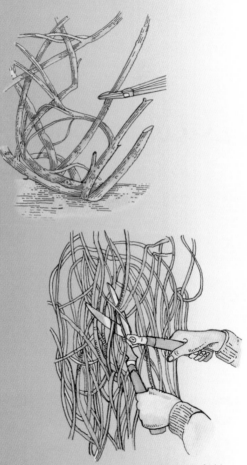

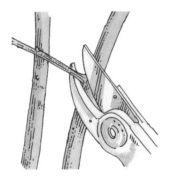

3 At the same time, cut back diseased shoots to strong and healthy shoots. If left, they will spread infection and disease.

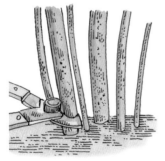

4 Some climbers continually develop new stems from their bases; the old ones eventually become thick, unproductive and congested. Use strong loppers to cut off these shoots at their base.

1 *If a honeysuckle becomes a total mass of old stems, in spring use secateurs or loppers to cut the complete plant to within 38–50cm (15–20in) of the ground.weight of their leaves and stems can often break their supports.***2** *Where it is just a mass of thin, tangled shoots, cut back the dead shoots from the base and use strong hand shears to trim thin shoots back to new growths.*

deciduous climbers & wall shrubs

Many of the wall shrubs included here can be grown as free-standing shrubs in sheltered gardens. However, growing them against walls is a useful way of increasing the number of plants that can be grown in a garden as well as providing some of the less tender species with valuable protection in winter. Some evergreen species are described on pages 60–61. Clematis are described on pages 62–5 and wisteria on pages 66–7.

suggested plants

Abutilon x suntense is a deciduous garden hybrid, which bears clusters of eyecatching violet-purple flowers from mid-spring to autumn. It grows to a height of 2m (6ft) with a spread of 1.5–1.8m (4–6ft). See also page 60.

Aristolochia macrophylla (syn. **A. durior**; Dutchman's pipe) is a tender, but strongly growing climber. Little pruning is needed, other than to shorten excessively long shoots by a third in late winter or early spring.

Campsis radicans (trumpet vine) is a vigorous North American climber, where it is also known as cow-itch and trumpet honeysuckle. In a warm, sheltered position it can grow up to 9m (30ft) high, but it is usually smaller. It adheres to supports by its aerial roots. The light green leaves have 9 or 11 leaflets, with orange and scarlet flowers appearing in terminal clusters in late summer and autumn. It is essential to cut back newly planted climbers to about 15cm (6in) high to encourage the development of shoots from the plant's base. Prune established plants in late winter or early spring, cutting shoots that were produced in the previous year to 5–8cm (2–3in) from the base.

Celastrus orbiculatus (bittersweet, staff vine) is a hardy, vigorous climber, growing to 10m (30ft). In early and midsummer it bears starry, greenish-yellow flowers. These are followed by glistening, orange-yellow fruits, while the leaves change from mid-green to clear yellow in autumn. When it is grown against a wall or on a pergola, thin out unwanted or misplaced shoots in early spring, and cut back main shoots by half. When it is growing up a tree it can be left alone.

Chaenomeles (Japanese quince, cydonia) is a genus of three hardy, spring-flowering shrubs that grow well on banks or against walls. When it is planted against a wall, cut back the previous season's growths in spring or early summer, after the flowers have faded, to within two or three buds of their base.

Chimonanthus praecox (wintersweet) can be grown against a wall, cut out all flowered shoots to within two buds of their base after the flowers fade.

Humulus lupulus 'Aureus' (yellow-leaved hop, golden hop) is a superb herbaceous climber, with bright yellow leaves. It is ideal for creating a screen to about 1.8m (6ft high). Each year all stems die down to ground level, and fresh shoots appear in spring; remove dead shoots in late autumn or early winter.

Hydrangea anomala subsp. **petiolaris (climbing hydrangea)** is hardy and vigorous, reaching 12m (40ft) or more when given a large tree to climb. Normally, it is less vigorous and looks superb when cascading up and over a high wall. In early summer it develops flat-headed clusters, to 25cm (10in) across, of creamy-white flowers. It needs no regular pruning, but cut out dead shoots in spring.

Jasminum nudiflorum (winter-flowering jasmine) is a slender shrub. After the flowers have faded in mid-spring cut out to within 5–8cm (2–3in) of ground level all shoots that produced flowers to encourage fresh shoots. At the same time, cut out weak and old shoots completely. After the white flowers of *J. officinale* (common jasmine) have faded, thin out flowered shoots to their bases. Do not just shorten them.

Lonicera spp. (honeysuckle) are among the best loved of all twining climbers are *L. periclymenum* 'Belgica' (early Dutch honeysuckle) creates a mass of purple-red and yellow flowers in early and midsummer. *L. periclymenum* 'Serotina' (late Dutch honeysuckle) has reddish-purple flowers with creamy-white insides from midsummer to autumn. No regular pruning of either is needed, other than occasionally cutting out old and congested shoots in spring.

Parthenocissus henryana (syn. Vitis henryana; Chinese Virginia creeper) needs no regular pruning; cut out dead or overcrowded shoots in spring. *P. quinquefolia* (syn. *Vitis quinquefolia*; Virginia creeper) and *P. tricuspidata* (Boston ivy) are pruned in the same way.

Schizophragma integrifolium is ideal for covering a pergola, wall or tree trunk, where it attaches itself by aerial roots. It often grows 6m (20ft) high and from midsummer to autumn displays 30cm (12in) wide clusters of

Left: The bright yellow-green leaves of *Humulus lupulus* 'Aureus' (golden hop) contrast beautifully with the dark brick wall and wooden bench.
Above: *Hydrangea anomala* subsp. *petiolaris* (climbing hydrangea) is a vigorous climber which looks particularly effective growing against a wall.

small white flowers surrounded by white bracts, each to 8cm (3in) or more long. *S. hydrangeoides* has creamy-white flowers and pale yellow bracts. Cut dead flowers and unwanted shoots from wall-trained plants in autumn. Plants that are climbing into trees can be left alone.

Vitis coignetiae (Japanese crimson glory vine) is a vigorous deciduous climber with tendrils. It is ideal for covering large walls, fences and old tree stumps. The mid-green leaves with heart-shaped bases and three or five pointed lobes are often 30cm (12in) wide, and they turn brilliant scarlet and crimson in autumn. Some specimens have been known to grow 25m (80ft) high, clinging to old buildings and climbing into large trees. No regular pruning is needed, except to attempt to restrict growth by cutting out old shoots in late summer. At the same time, shorten young growths.

evergreen climbers
& wall shrubs

In mild areas plants described as semi-evergreen may be regarded as evergreen, especially when they are afforded protection by being grown against a wall. In mild areas, many of the wall shrubs listed opposite can be grown as specimens in the border. Evergreen climbers and wall shrubs are especially useful in the garden, as they provide year-round interest and colour. Hardy climbers like ivy can be relied on to disguise ugly walls and fences even in winter.

suggested plants

Abutilon (flowering maple) is a genus of tender deciduous and evergreen shrubs. They are best grown against the protection of a warm wall. Shorten frost-damaged and straggly shoots in mid-spring. Tie the main shoots to a framework of wires or canes.

Acacia spp. (wattle), which are native to Australia and Tasmania, flourish in temperate regions when planted against a warm, sheltered wall. Once the framework is formed, little attention is needed.

Akebia quinata (chocolate vine) is a semi-evergreen climber, with leaves formed of five leaflets. In spring it develops dark purple flowers, followed by dark purple, sausage-shaped fruits. Even when not bearing flowers, this climber is very attractive. Little pruning is needed, other than to cut out excessively long or dead shoots in sp ring. It needs little training as the twining shoots soon clamber over supports.

Berberidopsis corallina (coral plant) is a slightly tender climber, best grown against a wall. No regular pruning is needed but cut out dead shoots in late winter or early spring. This plant is native to Chile and should be planted in a cool, sheltered, slightly shaded position. The soil can be acid or neutral but should preferably be light, well-drained and sandy.

Carpenteria californica is an evergreen shrub best grown against a warm wall. No regular pruning is needed, but cut out straggly shoots after the flowers have faded.

Ceanothus (Californian lilac) evergreen varieties grow best against a warm, sheltered wall. These include *C. rigidus* (Monterey ceanothus), *C. impressus* (Santa Barbara ceanothus), *C.* 'Burkwoodii' and *C.* 'Cascade'. Little pruning is needed, but shorten the previous year's growths in spring.

Eccremocarpus scaber (Chilean glory flower) is not reliably hardy. In late spring cut out frost-damaged shoots. If the plant is severely damaged by frost, cut all stems to their bases in spring to encourage the development of fresh shoots.

Hedera (ivy) is a large and useful genus of reliable climbers. There are many attractive species and cultivars. *H. canariensis* 'Gloire de Marengo' (syn. *H. canariensis* 'Variegata'; Canary Island ivy) is a popular evergreen climber, which eventually forms a dense screen of large, dark green leaves that merge to silvery-grey edged in creamy-white. Plants are usually left to grow naturally, but if left completely alone for several years they may block gutters and penetrate cracks and crevices. In late winter or early spring of every year, therefore, check and cut back invasive shoots. Also cut back long stems in late summer. *H. colchica* 'Dentata Variegata' is another evergreen climber, with pale green, oval or heart-shaped leaves, about 20cm (8in) long, with creamy-yellow edges that later become creamy-white. Prune in the same way as recommended for *H. canariensis*. *H. helix* 'Oro di Bogliasco' (syn. *H. helix* 'Goldheart') is a superb small-leaved, variegated ivy for clambering up walls. The dull green leaves are irregularly splashed with yellow. It is self-supporting and needs little attention once established. When planted to scale a sunny wall it has a tendency to grow rapidly, but excess shoots can be removed in autumn.

Lapageria rosea (Chilean bellflower) is only half-hardy in temperate regions and must be planted against a warm, sunny wall. After the flowers have faded in late summer or early autumn thin out weak growths.

Lonicera japonica (Japanese honeysuckle) is semi-evergreen in some areas. No regular pruning is needed, other than occasionally thinning out congested plants in spring. *L. japonica* 'Aureoreticulata' is susceptible to frosts and may lose its leaves. No regular pruning is needed, other than occasionally thinning out old shoots after the flowers fade.

Passiflora caerulea (common passion flower) is a spectacular but not reliably hardy climber, with 8cm (3in) wide, white and blue flowers. From early to late summer supports are arrayed in flowers. In early or mid-spring, cut out tangled shoots to soil level or the main stems. Spur back sideshoots to a growth bud 15cm (6in) from the main stems.

Solanum crispum (Chilean potato tree) has a bushy, scrambling nature and grows about 5m (15ft) high. From early to late summer it bears 8–15cm (3–6in) wide clusters of star-shaped, purple-blue flowers about 2.5cm (1in) across and with prominent yellow anthers. *S. crispum* 'Glasnevin' is hardier and more freely flowering. The only pruning that is necessary is to trim back the previous season's growth in mid-spring to 15cm (6in) long. Also, cut out any weak shoots, and those that have been killed by frost. In spring think out weak shoots of *S. jasminoides* (potato vine) and cut out those damaged by frost.

Trachelospermum jasminoides (star jasmine, confederate jasmine) is a woody, twining climber. In early and mid-spring, thin out vigorous shoots to restrict excessively rampant plants.

Above left: Trachelospermum jasminoides (star jasmine), with its fragrant, star-shaped flowers, is ideal for any sheltered garden. *Right*: Although Eccremocarpus scaber (Chilean glory flower) is not reliably hardy, it is worth growing for its exotic orange-red flowers

clematis

The pruning instructions recommended for clematis are often complicated and confusing. This need not be so, for these climbers can be separated into just three groups, according to the age of each plant's shoots when they bear flowers.

Pruning group 1 contains early-flowering species and hybrids that bear flowers from late spring to midsummer on shoots produced in the previous year. This means that in any one year, as well as flowering on the previous year's growth, the plant is also producing shoots that will bear flowers later in the same year, creating a second and welcome flush of colour in late summer and sometimes into early autumn.

Pruning group 2 is formed of vigorous spring- and early summer-flowering types that bear flowers on short shoots that arise from growths that developed in the previous year and on the tips of the current season's growth.

Pruning group 3 includes the late-flowering, large-flowered cultivars, some small-flowered cultivars and late-flowering species. These clematis bear flowers in summer and autumn on shoots produced in the same season. Clematis in this group begin new growth in spring each year by developing fresh, young shoots from the ends of old shoots. If these plants are left unpruned, therefore, the bases of the plants will soon become bare and unsightly.

GROUP 1

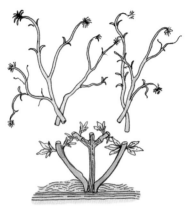

1 In late winter of the first year after planting prune plants by cutting the stem to slightly above the lowest pair of healthy, strong buds. This severe pruning encourages the development of strong shoots that will help to form the climber's framework. In summer space out and secure these stems to a permanent framework of wires or a wooden trellis. The initial training of shoots is important to ensure that light and air are able to reach the shoots.

2 In the late winter of the second year, cut back by half the lengths of the main shoots that developed in the previous year and were secured to a supporting framework. Make sure that each shoot is cut back to slightly above a pair of strong, healthy buds. If shoots low down on the climber develop flowers early in the year, cut them back to one pair of buds from their base. In the summer fresh shoots will grow; space these out and secure them to the supporting framework.

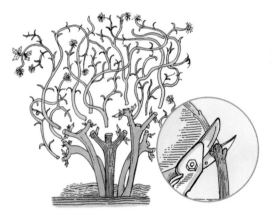

3 In early summer of the following and subsequent years, use secateurs to cut back all growths that produced flowers earlier in the year to one or two buds from their point of origin. Within this group, *C. montana* and *C. montana* var. *sericea* are very vigorous and sometimes left unpruned. This eventually creates a tangled plant. Rejuvenate by cutting to near ground level in late winter. When these two clematis are allowed to scale trees, leave them unpruned.

Group 1 clematis

Clematis in this group include:
- C. alpina *and cvs. such as* 'Frances Rivis'
- C. armandii *and cvs. such as* 'Apple Blossom'
- C. cirrhosa
- C. macropetala *and cvs such as* 'Markham's Pink'
- C. montana *f.* grandiflora, C. montana *var.* sericea, C. montana *var.* rubens *and cvs. such as* 'Alexander', 'Elizabeth' *and* 'Tetrarose'

GROUP 2

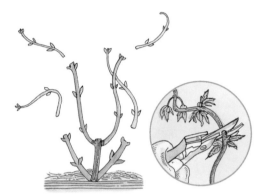

1 In the late winter after planting, cut back the stem to the lowest pair of strong, healthy buds. In late spring and early summer, young shoots will grow rapidly and need to be trained and secured to a framework of wires or a wooden trellis. Shoots will also develop from ground level and these, too, should be trained to the framework. Occasionally, a few flowers are produced in the first year.

2 In late winter of the second year, cut back by half all the main shoots which were produced in the previous year. Sever them just above a pair of strong, healthy buds. In the following summer, train the new shoots and space them out on the supporting framework. In this second season, plants usually develop a few flowers on new growth, often into autumn. Creating a strong framework of shoots is essential.

Group 2 clematis

Clematis in this group include:
- *Florida group cvs such as 'Duchess of Edinburgh' and 'Vyvyan Pennell'*
- *Lanuginosa group hybrids such as 'Carnaby', 'Elsa Späth', 'Général Sikorski', 'Marie Boisselot' and 'Nelly Moser'*
- *Patens group hybrids. such as 'Barbara Jackman', 'Daniel Deronda', 'Lasurstern', 'Mrs N. Thompson' and 'The President'*
- *Other large-flowered cvs such as 'Henryi' and 'Niobe'*

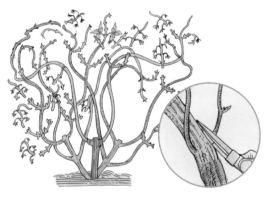

3 In early and midsummer of the third and subsequent years, immediately after the first flush of flowers have faded, cut out a quarter to a third of mature shoots to within 30cm (12in) of the plant's base. When plants are grown against a wall, the shoots can be readily reached and the above pruning is ideal. However, when grown on a pergola, stems cannot be untangled and plants are therefore best left unpruned.

GROUP 3

1 In late winter after planting, cut back the main shoot to the lowest pair of strong buds. Rigorously cutting back the plant in this way encourages the development of fresh shoots. in the following summer, healthy young shoots develop and must be trained and secured against a wire or wooden framework. Pruning a clematis vigorously in this way encourages the development of strong shoots from ground level, creating a bushy plant.

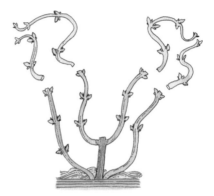

2 In late winter of the second year cut back each shoot to its lowest pair of strong buds. This also includes shoots that developed from ground level in the previous year and are starting to form a bushy plant. In the following summer vigorous shoots develop and, again, they must be spaced out and secured to a supporting framework. From mid- to late summer flowers will appear on shoots produced earlier in the same season.

3 In late winter of each subsequent year, cut all growths back to leave a pair of strong buds at their base. In the same way as in the previous years, shoots will grow from these buds and bear flowers from midsummer to autumn. Tie shoots to a framework. If a plant becomes neglected, cut half of the stems back into older wood to encourage the development of shoots from ground level; cut the others back to buds. The following year, cut back the other half.

Group 3 clematis

Clematis in this group include:
- *Jackmanii hybrids such as 'Comtesse de Bouchaud', 'Ernest Markham', 'Hagley Hybrid' and 'Perle d'Azur'*
- *C. florida and hybrids such as 'Flore Pleno'*
- *C. tangutica and hybrids such as 'Bill MacKenzie' and 'Golden Harvest'*
- *C. texensis and hybrids such as 'Duchess of Albany', 'Étoile Rose' and 'Gravetye Beauty'*
- *C. viticella and hybrids such as 'Ville de Lyon'*

PRUNING ESTABLISHED WISTERIA

Once a framework has been formed, the most important objective is to keep the climber in check: lateral shoots may grow to 3.6m (12ft) in a single year and unless this growth is pruned the plant can soon become a jungle of stems and too large for its allotted area. Severely pruning a wisteria in winter will encourage even more rapid growth. However, by cutting it in summer it is possible to restrain the plant without encouraging a massive amount of growth.

In late or early winter, cut back all shoots to within two or three buds of the point where they started growing in the previous season. Where a plant becomes too large, also prune it in midsummer, cutting the current season's young shoots back to within five or six buds of its base.

wisteria

Wisterias are perhaps the most spectacular and best-known flowering climbers for covering walls and pergolas or even climbing into trees. In late spring and early summer they are covered in pendulous clusters of fragrant blue or white pea-shaped flowers.

STANDARD WISTERIA

Wisterias are usually trained over pergolas and rustic poles or against walls, but an alternative and unusual approach is to train a single stem up a 1.8–2.1m (6–7ft) tall stake and then train branches over a wooden framework that radiates out and forms a flat-topped umbrella.

Start with a young plant and tie it to a strong stake. Train the shoot's tip upwards and at the same time allow sideshoots to develop. Cut them back to about 23cm (9in) long. Later, when the central shoot is 45-60cm (18-24in) above the top of the supporting framework, cut it off and allow sideshoots at the top to develop to form a canopy. Later, cut off all of the other sideshoots, close to the main stem.

When established, both summer and winter pruning is necessary to ensure the regular production of flowers and to curb an excessive amount of growth.

PRUNING YOUNG WISTERIA

Young wisterias need careful pruning and training to ensure a strong framework is created.

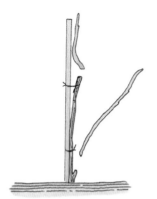

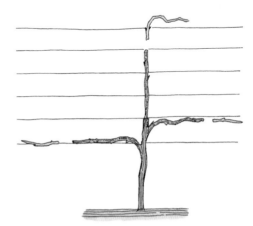

1 In late winter or early spring in the year after planting, cut back the strongest shoot to about 75cm (2½ft) above the ground. At the same time, completely cut off all other shoots.

2 In midwinter of the second year, cut back the central leading shoot to within 75–90cm (2½–3ft) of the topmost lateral shoot. At the same time, lower the laterals so that they are horizontal and cut them back by a third. Sever these lateral stems just beyond a bud on the upperside. Tie them to the wires.

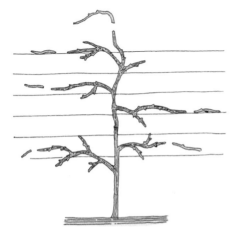

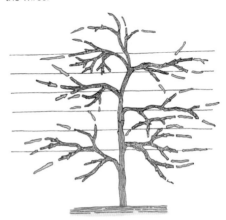

3 In winter of the third year, sever the central leading shoot to within 75–90cm (2½–3ft) of the uppermost horizontal stem. Then, lower the topmost horizontal shoots and cut them back by about a third. The lower horizontal shoots will have grown; cut off about a third of their new growth.

4 In subsequent winters, continue forming new tiers of horizontal shoots, as well as encouraging the growth of the leader shoot. When the desired height is reached, cut it off fractionally above the uppermost horizontal shoot. At the same time, cut back sideshoots to 8–10cm (3–4in) of their base.

4 TREES

Trees are often expected to grow without receiving any attention from one year to another. Many will, but a regular inspection at intervals throughout the year will certainly extend a tree's life. Strong winds and heavy snowfalls break and bend branches. In late winter remove any damaged, crossing or diseased branches. Some trees, such as *Prunus*, should be cut only when their sap is rising, but most can be pruned when they are dormant. It is easier to assess damage to deciduous trees in winter, when they are free from leaves. The pruning of many popular ornamental trees is described on pages 70–73.

Once they are established, neither broad-leaved nor coniferous trees need much pruning. During the formative years, however, it is essential that conifers are checked every year to make sure they have only one leading shoot. If two are allowed to grow, the conifer develops a forked top. This is unsightly and in some areas heavy snowfalls make the tops of the conifers split. Use sharp secateurs to cut out one of the forked shoots. If the conifer is young, temporarily tie the leading shoot to a cane. With most trees, however, once a framework of strong, well-spaced branches has been formed, there is very little to do apart from removing dead and diseased shoots and, occasionally, removing a low-growing branch so that it does not spoil the tree's symmetry.

Very old and prized trees may require more than just the

Left: A mature tree, like this beautiful *Crataegus monogyna* (hawthorn) is a bonus in any garden.

removal of an occasional branch. Branches may need to be propped up, while others may have cavities that need to be cleaned out and filled to prevent decay spreading and disease taking hold. This involves scraping back decayed wood to a sound base, painting the surface with a fungicidal wound paint and then filling the cavity and sealing the wound with cement. Provision must be made to make sure water seeping into the filled area can drain away.

As trees age, large branches often need to be supported, either by props placed underneath them or by giant, threaded, staple-like hooks secured by washers and nuts and then held by cables suspended from branches higher up. In the past large, dog-collar-like constructions of iron were bolted around a limb that needed support and, by means of an iron rod or chain, linked to a similar device on a higher branch. Apart from being cumbersome and unattractive to look at, the two 'dog-collars' eventually restrict the flow of sap to the ends of branches. The areas on either side of the band become swollen and, later, the branch has to be completely removed. Unless these bands can be adjusted every year, it is better to use props or staple-like hooks.

REMOVING A LARGE BRANCH

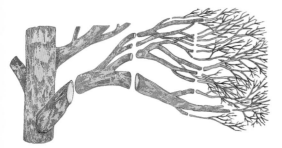

1 Cut off a large bough in several stages. Never cut it off close to the trunk in a single stage as the tree may be damaged. Cutting off a branch in several parts also creates pieces that are more manageable to move.

2 After a large branch has been cut back to about 45cm (18in) from the trunk, use a saw to cut two-thirds of the way through it from below. Position the cut close to the trunk, but not so near that it scrapes the bark. Making the first cut under the bough ensures that bark below the branch does not subsequently become damaged.

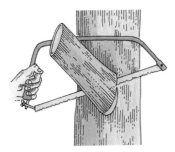

3 Cut through the remaining part of the branch from above. Position the saw so that the two cuts align and do not create a step. If they do not quite meet, use a coarse file to level them. If the two cuts are a long way out of alignment, it may be necessary to make a further cut to create a flat surface. Use a sharp saw – it makes the job easier.

4 Use a sharp knife to smooth the edges of the cut. If left rough, the cut both looks unattractive and extends the time the wound takes to heal. When smooth, coat the surface with a fungicidal wound paint to prevent diseases entering the tree and eventually causing extensive damage to the trunk.

Left: *Aralia elata* 'Variegata' (Japanese angelica tree) is grown for its distinctive leaves, which have creamy-white margins. The tiny white flowers are borne in late summer.
Above: *Syringa vulgaris* 'Masséna' (lilac) creates a showy display.

pruning deciduous trees

Occasionally an established tree has to be pruned because it has become too large and intrudes on other plants or into a neighbour's garden. When you choose a tree, find out how big it will be after 15–20 years before you buy. The deciduous trees listed opposite are suitable for most gardens. Some evergreen trees are described on pages 72–3. The ultimate height of each tree grown in ideal conditions is indicated. Some genera – *Ilex* (holly) and *Magnolia*, for example – include both deciduous and evergreen species. They are included among the evergreens.

suggested plants

Acer japonicum (Japanese maple) is a spreading deciduous shrub or small tree to 10m (30ft). Prune to shape when young and occasionally remove congested shoots. Prune in late summer or early autumn to prevent bleeding. Small forms of *A. palmatum*, to 8m (25ft), have dissected leaves with brilliant autumn colours. Prune lightly, in the same way as *A. japonicum*. *A. p.* 'Dissectum Atropurpureum' has deeply dissected, deep red leaves and a domed, slightly pendulous outline; it grows to about 75cm (2½ft) high and 1.5m (5ft) wide. *A. shirasawanum* 'Aureum', a yellow-leaved form of Japanese maple, is slow-growing and eventually reaches 4.5–6m (15–20ft) high. The leaves assume rich crimson tints before falling.

Aralia elata (Japanese angelica tree) is a vigorous deciduous tree which grows to 10m (30ft). No regular pruning is needed, but it sends up suckers, and if it spreads excessively cut out shoots to ground level in spring.

Betula spp. (birch) are deciduous trees, some species of which grow to 20m (70ft). No regular pruning is needed. Where a misplaced branch needs to be removed, cut it out in late autumn when there is less chance of it bleeding.

Cercis siliquastrum (Judas tree) is a deciduous tree to 10m (30ft). No regular pruning is needed, other than shaping when the plant is young and, later, removing dead shoots in spring when mature. *C. chinensis* (Chinese redbud), to 6m (20ft), is pruned in exactly the same way as *C. siliquastrum*. It bears a wealth of bright pink, pea-type flowers in late spring and early summer and is ideal for planting as a focal point in a large lawn. The bare trunk, often to 1.2m (4ft) high, allows bulbous plants to be grown under it.

Cornus spp. (dogwoods) are small deciduous trees, to 6m (10ft) depending on species. When they are grown as trees, dogwoods need no regular pruning, other than occasionally cutting them back in late winter to prevent them from intruding on neighbouring plants.

Ginkgo biloba (maidenhair tree), a deciduous tree to 30m (100ft), should not be pruned because it may cause shoots to die back.

Larix spp. (larch) are coniferous deciduous trees to 30m (100ft). They require no pruning, but make sure that each tree has only one leading shoot.

Malus spp. (crab apple) requires no regular pruning but make sure that crossing, diseased, damaged or misplaced branches are cut out in late winter.

Metasequoia glyptostroboides (dawn redwood) is a deciduous coniferous tree, growing to 40m (130ft). No pruning is needed, except to ensure that there is only one leading shoot.

Prunus is a large genus which includes a wide range of ornamental shrubs and trees (see pages 100–109 for fruit-bearing *Prunus* species). These vary in the treatment required.

Ornamental almonds need no regular pruning, but cut back the old, flowered shoots of *P. glandulosa* and *P. triloba* immediately after their flowers have faded, trimming them to within two or three buds of the previous season's wood. Ornamental cherries require no regular pruning, but if large branches need to be removed do this in late summer. When *P. incisa* (Fuji cherry) is grown as a hedge it must be clipped immediately after its flowers fade. One of the best of the Japanese cherries is *P.* 'Kanzan', which is grown for its coppery-red, young leaves and large clusters of purple-pink, double flowers. It is vigorous and eventually forms a large tree. *P. padus* 'Watereri' (bird cherry) develops almond-scented, white flowers in tail-like clusters up to 20cm (8in) long in late spring and into early summer. Eventually it grows to 15m (50ft), so it needs plenty of space. Plant it where the fragrance, flower shape and colour can be admired.

Neither ornamental peaches nor ornamental plums need regular pruning, but when they are used for hedges *P. x blireana*, *P. x cistena* and *P. cerasifera* (myrobalan) can be clipped at any time when they are not in flower.

Pyrus salicifolia 'Pendula' **(willow-leaved pear)** is a weeping tree, to 5m (15ft). No regular pruning is needed, but occasionally thin out overcrowded branches and shorten long, straggly growths in late summer.

Salix (willow) is a large genus, and some species, including *S. babylonica* (weeping willow), can grow quite large. No regular pruning is needed for the tree forms, other than occasionally cutting out dead shoots during winter. However, several species are grown for their coloured stems, such as *S. alba* subsp. *vitellina* and *S. alba* subsp. *vitellina* 'Britzensis', and these are completely cut back to within 5–8cm (2–3in) of the ground in late winter or early spring.

Sorbus spp. (mountain ash) are attractive trees, to 6m (20ft) or more, which require no regular pruning. Thin out or shape trees in winter after the fruits have fallen. In addition, cut out obstructive branches that have become too low.

Syringa spp. (lilac) create eye-catching, pyramidal spires of flowers, mainly in spring and early summer. The range of cultivars is wide and includes plants bearing white, pink or purplish-red flowers, some single, double. Some of them are superbly scented. Each year, use secateurs to cut off faded flowers. In winter cut out weak and crossing branches.

Where lilacs have been neglected, rejuvenate them by cutting the entire plant back to 60–90cm (2–3ft) above the ground in mid-spring. However, bear in mind that it will then be two or three years before flowers are produced. In summer remove any suckers which are growing from the main stem.

Tamarix spp. (tamarisk) are shrubs and small trees to about 5m (15ft). Prune the spring-flowering *T. tetrandra* immediately the flowers have faded. Cut back by half to two-thirds of the previous season's growth. Prune the late summer-flowering *T. ramosissima* (syn. *T. pentandra*) in late winter or early spring, again cutting back the previous season's shoots by half to two-thirds.

Left: An elegant standard *Laurus nobilis* (bay) surrounded by a neat *Buxus* (box) hedge.
Above: *Arbutus unedo* (strawberry tree) has attractive flowers and fruit.
Top right: *Ilex x altaclarensis* 'Golden King' (variegated holly) should be shaped in spring.

pruning evergreen trees

Evergreen trees provide interest and form all year round in the garden, and some of the most widely grown are described here. There are, of course, many suitable trees, but it is extremely important to consider the ultimate size of the tree when you are making your choice.

Some of the evergreen shrubs which have been suggested for hedges on pages 83 and 85 will, if left unpruned, eventually assume tree-like proportions. In temperate areas evergreen trees are mostly conifers, which require little attention once they are established.

suggested plants

Abies spp. (silver fir) is an evergreen conifer, growing to 20m (65ft) or more high, although there are some dwarf forms, such as *A. balsamea* Hudsonia Group. Make sure you choose an appropriate species for your garden. Little pruning is needed, other than to make sure that young plants do not have two leading shoots. In spring, use sharp secateurs to remove one of the shoots, as well as sideshoots near the leading shoot.

Araucaria araucana (monkey puzzle tree) requires no pruning, which spoils this conifer's outline. Mature trees grow to 25m (80ft).

Arbutus unedo (strawberry tree) needs no regular pruning, but straggly shoots should be cut out in spring. In addition, branches that obscure the trunks of trees grown for their attractive bark should be removed. These evergreen trees grow to 8m (25ft).

Calocedrus decurrens (syn. Libocedrus decurrens; incense cedar) is a narrow, upright, coniferous evergreen to 40m (130ft). No pruning is needed except to make sure that only a single leading shoot is present.

Cedrus spp. (cedar) are large conifers, some to 40m (130ft), which require no regular pruning, but make sure there is only one leading shoot. Cut off old branches in late winter or early spring, but take care not to spoil the tree's outline.

Chamaecyparis spp. (false cypress) are upright coniferous evergreens, to 40m (130ft), although many dwarf and compact cultivars are available. They need no regular pruning, but make sure that leading shoots do not fork. Prune in mid-spring when necessary.

Cryptomeria (Japanese cedar), a coniferous evergreen to 10m (30ft), needs no regular pruning. Make sure that plants do not develop two leading shoots. Prune one of them out in spring.

x Cupressocyparis leylandii (syn. Cupressus leylandii; Leyland cypress) is a large coniferous evergreen, which can grow to 35m (120ft). Once plants are established with a single leading shoot little further pruning is needed. Prune in spring if it is necessary to control the plant's size.

Cupressus spp. (cypress) are evergreen conifers that need no regular pruning, other than to ensure there is only one leading shoot. Prune in spring. The larger species can reach heights of 30m (100ft).

Ilex spp. (holly), which can be either deciduous or evergreen and can grow to 15m (50ft), need no regular pruning other than cutting them to shape them in spring. Excessively large or straggly plants can be cut back hard in late spring. Variegated hollies are superb for creating colour all year. *Ilex aquifolium* (common holly) has many variegated forms. Some of them, such as *I. aquifolium* 'Ferox Argentea', have leaves with both variegation and puckered, spiny surfaces.

Juniperus spp. (juniper) evergreen conifers, need no pruning is needed. Make sure there is only one leading shoot. The species are very variable; some grow to 20m (70ft), while some dwarf forms are to60cm (2ft).

Laurus nobilis (bay), an evergreen to 12m (40ft), is grown as specimen bushes and standards in borders and large tubs. It needs clipping with secateurs two or three times in summer. Rejuvenate neglected and old shrubs in late spring by cutting them back severely.

Magnolia spp. Deciduous types do not need pruning. Indeed, they resent being cut as wounds do not readily heal. However, prune the evergreen *M. grandiflora* in spring. *M. x soulangeana* forms a spreading tree or large shrub, to 6m (20ft), bearing white, chalice-shaped flowers to 15cm (6in) across in spring, before the leaves appear. Before opening, the flowers are stained rose-purple at their base.

Picea (spruce) are coniferous evergreens, which can grow to 40m (130ft), and they make handsome specimen plants. No regular pruning is needed, other than to ensure that there is just one leading shoot.

Pinus (pine). This genus contains

more than 100 species, with a wide range of habits and leaf colour. Some species grow to over 30m (100ft) high, but several compact forms, especially of *P. mugo* (dwarf mountain pine) are available. No pruning is needed, except to ensure that there is only one leading shoot. If the central shoot becomes damaged, remove all but the strongest shoot from the growth below.

Prunus laurocerasus (cherry laurel) is an evergreen shrub, which will become tree-like if left unpruned, eventually growing to 8m (25ft). There are many attractive cultivars. Use secateurs to cut back large plants in late spring or early summer.

Taxus spp. (yew) need no regular pruning needed but clusters of sucker-like shoots should be cut from the tree's trunk. This can be done at any time of the year. Yews are grown for their dark foliage, and in small gardens, fastigiate forms can be planted to provide upright emphasis.

Thuja spp. (arborvitae) need no pruning, although it is important that there is only one leading shoot.

Tsuga spp. (hemlock) are evergreen coniferous trees, with a wide range of leaf colour. Large species will grow to 20m (65ft) or more, but several more compact cultivars are available. No regular pruning is needed, but make sure there is only one leading shoot.

5 HEDGES & TOPIARY

Hedges have both a functional and an aesthetic role in a garden. In the Middle Ages they were solely used to keep out wandering animals and people, while miniature box hedges were later used to create neat, raised edges to borders. Today many of the hedges planted along the perimeters of gardens still have a defensive nature, especially when clipped to form crenellations, but there are also informal hedges, some abounding in flowers, others with attractive leaves. Internal hedges, perhaps separating one part of a garden from another or just acting as a decorative feature along a path, are also popular, and *Lavandula* (lavender) forms an attractive and scented internal hedge. Whatever the nature and purpose of a hedge, however, early pruning while the plants become established and regular attention later are essential.

Bottom left: Buxus sempervirens (box) clipped into a pyramid shape adds interest and height to this border.
Left: Fagus sylvatica f. *purpurea* (copper beech) is used to create decorative internal boundaries.

The range of hedges is wide, but, basically, those with a formal outline are usually grown for their foliage and informal types with irregular shapes are planted for their beautiful leaves or flowers. Some of these hedging and screening plants are evergreen conifers; others are shrubs and may be either deciduous or evergreen.

For many years in the middle part of the 20th century, the all-green or golden-leaved *Ligustrum* spp. (privet) were mainly used to form hedges. Although they still have a role in gardens, there are many other hedging plants to consider. Evergreen shrubs and conifers with attractive foliage are still the most popular plants for hedges,

although increasingly flowering shrubs are being employed. Part of this change of allegiance from the use of privet has been the trend away from 'boxed-off' front gardens to open-plan designs. If a defensive or view-blocking hedge is not needed, a front garden with a width of 9m (30ft) can save up to 8.5sq m (90sq ft) of space. This is because a privet hedge, when overgrown, can easily form a barrier 90cm (3ft) thick. Such hedges also impoverish soil around them. Nevertheless, alongside roads and in cold, wind-exposed areas they are invaluable for deadening noise and giving protection against wind. In exposed areas, evergreen hedges are frequently the first features to be

established in gardens.

There are flowering hedges for boundaries as well as decorative internal ones. For many years *Crataegus monogyna* (hawthorn) was used to create hedges in rural areas, where its thorns prevented the entry of animals and its white, heavily scented flowers provided a welcome display in late spring and early summer. It still has its uses, but in urban gardens the evergreen and winter-flowering *Viburnum tinus* (laurustinus) creates an attractive feature from late autumn to late spring or early summer (see pages 78–9).

In countries with a Mediterranean climate *Hibiscus rosa-sinensis* (Chinese hibiscus) forms a spectacular hedge, but colourful flowers are possible in temperate regions, with escallonias, lavender, shrubby potentilla, rhododendrons, roses and rosemary all creating bright, highly scented screens.

Topiary, the art of shaping shrubs, trees and evergreen conifers, has been known for about 2000 years, although there have been periods when it was not popular in fashionable circles. Nevertheless, it persisted in cottage gardens and has recently became a popular art form again. Some simple guidelines are included on pages 86–7.

regular maintenance

Above: This *Ligustrum* (privet) hedge is in need of trimming. Small-leaved hedging like this is usually trimmed with hand shears.

Hedges are often the most neglected plants in a garden, but they actually need as much attention in their infancy as other plants, as well as continued clipping and training in their adult life. Hedges should also be fed, as you would feed other shrubs in your beds and borders.

Many shrubs and conifers can be encouraged to form hedges, either as a boundary alongside a road or to divide one part of a garden from another – or even as a decorative feature, such as in a knot garden, where dwarf hedges line paths and beds of herbs or flowers. Evergreen, semi-evergreen and deciduous plants can all be used.

In addition to shrubs and conifers, wonderful informal screens can be made from bamboos, which will eventually form dense thickets without the need for any pruning, except as a remedial treatment should they become damaged. *Pseudosasa japonica* (arrow bamboo), for instance, grows to 4.5m (15ft) high, and has dark, glossy green leaves. *Fargesia nitida* (syn. *Arundinaria nitida*; fountain bamboo) is less vigorous and has purple stems and bright green leaves. For a lower hedge, *Sasa veitchii* is a better choice: it forms a dense thicket to 1.2m (4ft) high. The large, green leaves have light, straw-coloured edges. The only pruning necessary with bamboos is to cut out stems that have been damaged after heavy falls of snow have been allowed to remain on top of them for several days.

Formal hedges, on the other hand, usually have clean, crisp outlines, and they are invariably formed of evergreen conifers, small-leaved evergreen shrubs or deciduous shrubs, such as *Fagus sylvatica* (beech), *Carpinus betulus* (hornbeam) and *Crataegus monogyna* (hawthorn), which can all be clipped back to smooth, neat lines.

ESTABLISHING A FORMAL HEDGE

1 Deciduous, formal hedging plants must be cut down by about half and have all sideshoots cut back by a similar amount immediately after being planted. When bought as bare-rooted plants, planting is from late autumn to early spring. For container-grown plants, you can plant them at any time when the soil is workable.

2 In the following year, from late autumn to early spring, again severely cut back the leading shoot and sideshoots by about a half. This may appear to be too drastic and to lose much of the plant, but unless pruning is severe the base of the hedge will be unsightly and bare of stems and leaves in summer.

3 In the third winter, cut back all new shoots by a third. In the following season, shoots that develop will be bushy and start to form a solid screen of leaves. During a hedge's infancy, remember to water it regularly and feed it in spring and midsummer to encourage the development of young shoots.

SHAPING A HEDGE

Creating a uniform shape along a hedge's entire length is essential. To establish a uniform height, a taut string stretched between stout poles is ideal over a short distance, but a better way is to use a template, which can be made from sturdy cardboard or, for extensive hedges, from hardboard.

Left: Buxus sempervirens (box) is among those hedging plants that can be severely cut back.
Right: Ribes sanguineum (flowering currant) makes a colourful informal hedge.

renovating old hedges

Hedges in old gardens often become neglected, too large and bare of shoots and stems at their bases. They encroach into the beds and borders they screen and swamp neighbouring plants. They also impoverish the soil, as well as obscuring the light and becoming full of old, dusty leaves and stems. They also often harbour weeds. However, it is frequently possible to renovate such a neglected hedge.

If the hedge is too wide it can be cut back hard in spring. Often, however, this may be too drastic to do all at once, and it is generally better to spread the work over two or three seasons. In the first year, cut back the top to the desired height, using a line to get a uniform height. In the second year, prune back hard one of the sides. The following year, cut the other side back hard. Hedging material is rarely suitable for the compost heap unless you have a shredder, and it is often better to burn it or take

Pruning small-leaved hedges

Small-leaved hedging, such as Ligustrum spp. (privet), is traditionally trimmed with hand shears. Modern hand shears are lighter to use than earlier models and do not judder wrists and hands so violently. Nevertheless, for many gardeners they are still difficult to use, especially on a large hedge. The alternative is to use an electrically powered trimmer: some cut on both sides of the blades, others on one only. Where the distance from a power supply is great, rechargeable types can be used. Use earmuffs to reduce the risk of damage to ears and wear goggles to protect your eyes.

it to a municipal tip. When you have cleared away the cuttings and removed any weeds that were growing at the base of the hedge, apply a fertilizer and, when the soil is damp, a mulch to encourage new shoots to develop and to keep down weeds at the base.

Not all hedging plants can be severely cut back and can be guaranteed to regrow, but those that can include *Aucuba japonica* (spotted laurel), *Fagus sylvatica* (common beech), *Buxus sempervirens* (box), *Elaeagnus* (deciduous forms), *Forsythia* x *intermedia*, *Ulex europaeus* (gorse), *Crataegus monogyna* (hawthorn), *Ligustrum ovalifolium* (privet), *Pyracantha* spp. (firethorn), *Rhododendron* cvs and *Taxus baccata* (yew).

Rosmarinus officinalis (rosemary) and *Lavandula angustifolia* (lavender) are often used for hedging, especially around herb gardens, but both eventually become tall and straggly, especially when they are not trimmed annually. New

growth will not develop when the pruning cuts have been made into the old wood, and, rather than cutting them back severely, they are best replaced with young plants. When you replace the plants, renew some of the soil at the same time. Prune the new, young plants in mid-spring to encourage them to adopt a neat, low habit, and every subsequent year remove 2–3cm

(1in) of the previous season's growth to encourage bushy, even growth.

With the exception of *Taxus baccata* (yew), overgrown conifers should not be drastically cut back as this will completely spoil them. However, the tops of conifers can be cut out from young hedges when the desired height has been reached (see pages 84–5).

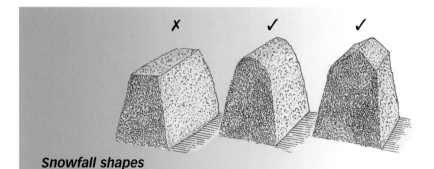

X   ✓   ✓

Snowfall shapes

Rain cleanses hedges of dust and dirt, but heavy snowfalls often cause irreparable damage because the weight breaks shoots and splays branches outwards. Instead of a square top, choose a rounded or a sloped outline, so that snow can more easily fall off. In warm areas, where there is little risk of snow, the top of a hedge can be cut with more of a square outline.

Left: A mixture of beeches
(*Fagus*) makes an
interesting contrast of
colours in this hedge.
Below: *Potentilla fruticosa*
'Katherine Dykes' (shrubby
cinquefoil) is covered in
primrose-yellow flowers
in summer.
Bottom right: Trim *Berberis*
into shape in winter.

deciduous hedging plants

Deciduous plants may not be
everyone's first choice for a
hedge. The year-round privacy
and screening provided by
evergreen plants means that
they are often selected
automatically when a boundary is
to be marked by a hedge. The
value of deciduous hedges
should not be overlooked,
however, especially when areas
within a garden are to be divided
by hedging. Some suitable plants
are described here, as well as
two of the most reliable and, for
many gardeners, the most
attractive hedging plants of all,
Fagus sylvatica (beech) and
Crataegus monogyna (hawthorn),
both of which are deciduous.

suggested plants

Berberis thunbergii (Japanese berberis) is a dense, round shrub. Trim it into shape with secateurs in winter, but wait until the berries have dropped. *B. thunbergii* 'Atropurpurea Nana' has reddish-purple leaves. Trim plants to shape with secateurs in winter. See page 83 for evergreen species.

Carpinus betulus (common hornbeam, European hornbeam) is a rather irregularly shaped plant, which will develop into a small tree if left to its own devices. Use hand shears to clip hedges to shape in midsummer.

Crataegus monogyna (common hawthorn) is also known as quick and may. It is a traditional hedging plant, whose thorns make it valuable if security is an important factor in your choice. Use hand shears to trim hedges to shape at any time after the flowers have faded and until late winter.

Where hedges have become neglected, cut them back in late summer – they will soon break into growth in the following year, even after having been cut severely.

Fagus sylvatica (beech) forms a moderately high, thick hedge, with superbly coloured leaves in autumn. Even when their colours fade, the marcescent leaves remain on the hedge for several months. Newly planted hedges must be immediately cut back by a half to a quarter to encourage the development of shoots from each plant's base. Once established, use hand shears or powered clippers to trim it to shape in mid- or late summer. The eventual size of beech often prevents its wider use, especially for elderly gardeners who are unable to climb ladders and, with safety, use electrical hedge clippers.

Hippophae rhamnoides (sea buckthorn) is a large shrub, which will develop into a small tree if left unpruned. In late summer, use secateurs to cut back any long, straggly shoots.

Potentilla fruticosa (shrubby cinquefoil) is a popular flowering shrub for the border, but it can also be planted as a hedge. Use secateurs to cut back the tips of shoots when the flowers have faded. Also cut out weak and old shoots at their bases to encourage the development of further stems. *P. fruticosa* 'Katherine Dykes' forms a dome-shaped shrub about 1.5m (5ft) high and wide. Throughout most of summer it is smothered in large, buttercup-like, primrose-yellow flowers, about 2.5cm (1in) across.

Prunus x cistena is an upright, rather slow-growing shrub with reddish-purple leaves and white flowers in spring. Use secateurs to trim to shape after the flowers have faded in late spring.

Rhododendron luteum is a deciduous azalea that produces a magnificent display of fragrant, yellow flowers in late spring and early summer. In autumn the matt green leaves assume shades of rich scarlet. Although it is often grown as a specimen shrub in a wild garden, it is even better when planted as a background hedge. Acid soil is essential. Although widely grown and seen by some gardeners as 'ordinary', it nevertheless seldom fails to create an attractive feature. No regular pruning is needed, other than cutting out dead or crossing branches after the flowers have faded.

Symphoricarpos x doorenbosii 'White Hedge' is a compact and fairly upright form of snowberry. Thin out overgrown hedges in winter. Use secateurs to trim established hedges to shape several times during the course of the summer.

Tamarix ramosissima (syn. *T. pentandra*; tamarisk) is ideal as a windbreak or hedging plant in coastal gardens in mild areas. To produce hedges that are bushy at their bases, cut newly planted plants to 30cm (12in) high. Later, use secateurs to cut out the tips of the sideshoots when they are 15cm (6in) long. Once established, use secateurs in late winter or early spring to cut back the previous season's shoots to within 15cm (6in) of the points from where they originated. Because tamarisk is usually grown as a hedge only in warm coastal areas, it can be pruned earlier than when it is grown inland as a specimen feature.

Left: This unusual double hedge of *Rosmarinus* (rosemary) and *Buxus* (box) is a distinctive feature in a formal garden.
Bottom right: Escallonia, with lavender and calluna planted in front, creates colourful informal hedging.

evergreen hedging plants

Some large-leaved evergreen hedges are formed of plants grown solely for their attractive leaves, such as the popular and widely grown *Aucuba japonica* (spotted laurel), while others like *Viburnum tinus* (laurustinus) are better known for their flowers.

Large-leaved evergreen shrubs, which invariably create informal hedges, need little initial pruning other than cutting back long shoots to just above a leaf joint. However, cutting back the tips to slightly above leaves encourages bushiness and the development

of stronger shoots. At the same time, cut out disease- or pest-damaged shoots. If, in the second season, large-leaved shrubs are not creating a bushy outline, cut a few shoots back in order to encourage the development of sideshoots.

Pruning large-leaved evergreens

Large-leaved evergreen shrubs must be pruned with sharp secateurs rather than hand shears, which will chop leaves in half and create an unattractive mess. Always cut shoots back to just above a leaf joint. Fresh shoots will develop and hide the cuts. Do not position the cut so that a short piece of stem is left. This is not only unsightly but it may also cause the onset of die-back.

suggested plants

Aucuba japonica (spotted laurel) does not usually need pruning, but use sharp and strong secateurs to cut back old stems in spring.

Berberis darwinii (Darwin's berberis) is a vigorous plant. In early summer, after the flowers have faded, use secateurs to cut back long stems to create an overall even shape and thickness. Prune the hybrid *B. x stenophylla* in the same way. It is a vigorous, evergreen shrub, with arching stems, narrow, deep green leaves and golden-yellow flowers in spring and early summer. It forms a large hedge, often 1.8m (6ft) high and 1.5m (5ft) wide, and is ideal in a semi-formal or informal setting. Although long stems can be pruned after the flowers fade, it never has a formal outline.

Buxus microphylla (small-leaved box) is a slow-growing plant, often used for hedges in herb or knot gardens. *B. sempervirens* 'Suffruticosa' is also compact and slow growing, forming neat, dwarf, evergreen hedges to 23–30cm (9–12in) high and 20–25cm (8–10in) wide, although unpruned plants can get to 1m (more than 3ft) tall. The glossy, round, green leaves form a superb edging along paths. Trim plants into shape with hand shears in late summer or wait until early autumn.

Cotoneaster lacteus is a dense shrub. Use secateurs to cut off long shoots after the flowers have faded. At the same time, cut back the current season's shoots to where berries are forming. *C. simonsii* is semi-evergreen (deciduous in cold areas), with an erect habit that is ideal for forming hedges. Use secateurs to trim hedges in late winter or early spring. Trim deciduous plants in late summer or early autumn.

Escallonia cvs. which are sometimes semi-evergreen, form dense hedges. Once the plants are established, shoots can he cut back hard after the flowers have faded. A more abundantly flowered hedge can be created by light trimming. *E.* 'Donard Seedling' is slightly tender but is ideal for a hedge in a mild climate. The long, arching branches bear apple-blossom-pink flowers in early and midsummer.

Ilex (holly) includes some species that make excellent windbreaks and hedges. Use secateurs to trim hedges of *I. x altaclerensis* in mid-spring. Cut neglected hedges back in spring. *I. aquifolium* (common holly) should be pruned in the same way as *I. x altaclerensis*. *I. aquifolium* 'Golden Queen' is a hardy shrub that will create a hedge to 3m (10ft) high and 1.2m (4ft) wide. The leathery, dark green, shiny leaves have golden edges.

Lavandula angustifolia (lavender) makes a lovely and fragrant informal hedge. Pinch out newly planted hedges to encourage sideshoots. Use garden shears to clip established hedges to shape in early or mid-spring. Prune straggly plants back quite heavily (see also page 79).

Ligustrum ovalifolium (common privet) hedges are a common sight. Once the hedge is established, use hand shears to clip over it several times in summer. *L. ovalifolium* 'Aureum' is slightly less vigorous than the all-green species, but it is evergreen in all but the coldest winters. It needs slightly harder pruning than the species in its formative years; once established clip it in the same way as the species. The glossy leaves are often completely yellow, although sometimes they have green centres. Where hedges are a mixture of green and yellow privet, use two yellow plants to one of green.

Lonicera nitida (Chinese honeysuckle) is another widely grown hedging plant. Cut back newly planted hedges by a half. In the following year clip the young growths several times. In subsequent years cut back new growths by a half. Treat *L. nitida* 'Baggesen's Gold' in the same way.

Prunus laurocerasus (cherry laurel) is a dense shrub. Use secateurs to trim back shoots in late spring or late summer. Where hedges have grown too large, cut them hard back in spring. Prune *P. lusitanica* (Portugal laurel) in the same way.

Pyracantha rogersiana (firethorn) is a spreading shrub with narrow, mid-green leaves and clusters of white flowers in early summer, followed by bright, orange-red berries in autumn and into winter. *P. rogersiana* 'Flava' has exceptionally attractive bright yellow berries. When planted, use secateurs to cut plants back by half and in the following summer pinch back young shoots by about 15cm (6in). Repeat this in the following year. When established, use secateurs to trim plants in early summer, but the farther back a plant is cut, the fewer berries it will subsequently bear.

Rosmarinus officinalis (rosemary) flowers mainly in late spring and early summer, but often continues to bloom sporadically until autumn. It forms a superb evergreen shrub, with aromatic, dark green leaves and mauve flowers. *R. officinalis* 'Miss Jessopp's Upright' is more vigorous and taller, with light blue flowers. Use secateurs to cut out dead shoots in early spring. Cut out straggly and misplaced shoots. If plants have become overgrown, cut back all shoots by half in mid-spring (see also page 79).

Viburnum tinus (laurustinus) requires no regular pruning other than using secateurs to cut out dead and misplaced shoots when the flowers have faded in spring.

coniferous hedging plants

Evergreen coniferous hedges, such as x *Cupressocyparis leylandii* (Leyland cypress), *Chamaecyparis lawsoniana* (Lawson cypress) and *Thuja plicata* (western red cedar), form superb hedges. Some of the most popular and useful hedging conifers are described opposite.

For pruning purposes, in general, when the leading shoots reach 15–30cm (6–12in) above the desired height, cut off their tops about 15cm (6in) below this point. This allows the hedge naturally to create a bushy and well-filled top at the desired height.

Right: Cultivars of *Chamaecyparis* (cypress) with different coloured leaves have been combined to create this beautiful, tapestry-effect hedge.
Above: *Taxus baccata* (yew) has been used as formal hedging for hundreds of years.

suggested plants

Chamaecyparis lawsoniana
(syn. **Cupressus lawsoniana**; **Lawson cypress**) is often used for hedging, and there are many cultivars, offering a wide range of colours and habits of growth. Once the plants are established, use hand shears or powered clippers as necessary. When you are attempting to limit the height, cut off the top about 15cm (6in) below the required point. This encourages sideshoots to form an attractive top at the desired height. Allowing plants to grow 60cm (2ft) or more above the desired height before they are cut back will result in a sparse top that, if seen from above, looks hideous. As with all conifers, therefore, always remember to limit the height of the plants while they are still small and able easily to reclothe their tops.

x Cupressocyparis leylandii
(syn. **Cupressus leylandii**; **Leyland cypress**) is not a suitable hedging plant for any but the very largest of gardens. If you have such a hedge and it is not already beyond your reach, use garden shears to clip it to shape in late summer or early autumn. When you are attempting to limit the height, cut off the top 15cm (6in) or more below the desired point. This will allow sideshoots to form an attractive top at the desired height. The yellow-leaved form, x *C. leylandii* 'Castlewellan' (syn. x *C. l.* 'Galway Gold'), is less vigorous than the all-green form and can be used to create a tall, thick windbreak. Prune it in the same way as the ordinary Leyland cypress.

Cupressus macrocarpa
(**Monterey cypress**) has a rather narrow, upright habit, which makes it ideal for hedging. Use hand shears to trim it in its early years. In subsequent years, little trimming is needed. When limiting its height, cut off the top about 15cm (6in) below the desired point to enable sideshoots to form and an attractive top to be created at the required height. The attractive *C. macrocarpa* 'Goldcrest' forms a tall hedge with rich yellow, feathery foliage.

Taxus baccata (common yew)
has been used for centuries to create evergreen hedges. The massed, narrow, dark green leaves create a superb foil and wind-sheltered area for other garden plants, especially those with a herbaceous nature. Start off with small plants, and when they are about 30cm (12in) high nip out the growing tips to encourage bushiness. This will be necessary several times during the early years. Later, clip with hand shears in late summer.

Thuja occidentalis (white cedar)
is an underrated plant with yellowish-green leaves. Use hand shears to trim plants in late summer. When you are limiting its height, cut off the top about 15cm (6in) below the desired point. This will enable sideshoots to form an attractive top at the desired height. *T. plicata* (western red cedar) can be used to create a formal hedge that can even be clipped to form arches. The pineapple-scented leaves are shiny and mid-green. Prune in the same way as *T. occidentalis*.

Left: A classical topiary form created from *Taxus baccata* (yew)
Below right: A topiary cockerel brings a whimsical note to the garden.

PLANTS TO TOPIARIZE

There are several small-leaved evergreens that can be used to form topiary subjects. One of the most reliable is *Buxus sempervirens* (box), a slow-growing plant with small, aromatic, glossy green leaves. It is ideal for forming birds and animals as well as geometric shapes to 1.2m (4ft) high. It grows very well in containers. There are several cultivars with variegated leaves.

Ligustrum ovalifolium (privet) has shiny, green leaves, but it can be semi-evergreen in cold regions. There is a golden-leaved form. Privet is not suitable for planting in containers. The leaves are larger than those of *Lonicera nitida* (shrubby honeysuckle). This is a prolific grower with small, shiny, dark green leaves clustered around stiff stems. It is ideal for subjects up to 75cm (2ft 6in) high and long. The cultivar *L. nitida* 'Baggesen's Gold' has golden leaves. Both forms can be grown in tubs.

Taxus baccata (yew) is a small-leaved evergreen conifer bearing dark green leaves. It forms topiary subjects to 2.4m (8ft) high and will grow quite happily in containers.

Thuja occidentalis (arborvitae) and its many cultivars are evergreen conifers, which are ideal for simple topiary sculptures and also suitable for growing in containers. It can be used for topiary subjects to 1.5m (5ft) high.

topiary techniques

There is a certain romance about topiary, whether it is seen in a classical setting and depicts various geometric shapes or in a cottage garden, where a peacock has been created out of *Buxus sempervirens* (box) or *Lonicera nitida* (shrubby honeysuckle). Topiary does not have to be on the grand scale to be fun: a small sphere is just as satisfying for a novice as a more ambitious animal shape for an experienced enthusiast. In earlier times large-leaved evergreens, such as

Laurus spp. (laurel), were used, but this created features too large for cottage and other small gardens. Also, laurel is difficult to clip without damaging the leaves. Topiary is usually created from evergreen shrubs, but deciduous shrubs, such as forsythia and laburnums, can be used. A standard forsythia in spring is an unforgettable sight, but it does not have the year-round attraction of evergreens, especially those fashioned in the image of birds and animals.

CREATING A SIMPLE SHAPE

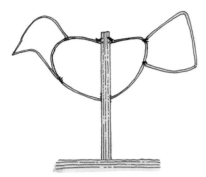

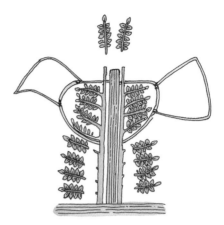

1 Never be too ambitious to begin with: an identifiable sphere, cone or small bird is better than a deformed kangaroo. Topiary experts are often able to create simple forms without the aid of a wire outline, but novices should use a 'former', which is best put in place before setting the plants in position. Secure the framework – not longer than 90cm (3ft) – to a strong stake.

2 Put a suitable plant on each side of the wooden stake. Loosely tie them to the stake and train them upwards until their tops are about 23cm (9in) above the framework. Then, preferably in spring, cut them level with the top of the framework. Cut off the lower shoots close to the stem. Select three or four shoots on each plant. Grow them vertically, shorten by a third and then train horizontally.

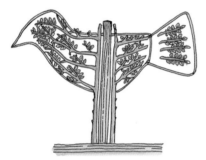

3 When the horizontal shoots have grown about 15cm (6in) past the main body, cut them back. Cutting the stems back radically each time encourages the development of stronger shoots more than if just their tips were removed. Do not be in a hurry for shoots to reach the ends of the framework. It is much more important to build up a strong internal body of shoots that are both firm and mature.

Making simple topiary shapes

Simple shapes, such as a cone formed by a conifer, perhaps Taxus baccata (yew) or Thuja occidentalis (arborvitae) are best for beginners. Use only one plant, tie it to a support and when a shoot reaches about 15cm (6in) above the top cut it off. Trim it to shape regularly.

6 FRUIT TREES

Fruit gardens are a medley of trees, bushes and canes, some with a permanent framework, others with a woody structure that is replaced each year. Most of these plants are free-standing, creating bushes or trees with only a single stake to support them. Others, such as cordons, espaliers and fans, need tiered wires strained between posts or secured to a wall. Because space in most gardens is limited, few standard and half-standard apple and pear trees are now planted; instead, bushes or forms trained against a wall are more popular.

Fruit gardens in temperate countries yield as many succulent fruits as those in tropical regions, and there is the additional advantage that many of them keep for longer in storage. This is especially true of apples, some varieties of which, although picked in the late summer or autumn of one year, can be stored for eating well into the following year.

To encourage the annual production of fruit on trees, yearly pruning is essential, and it is especially needed where fruit trees are trained to grow against walls or alongside frameworks of supporting wires. Growing fruit trees at angles of 45 degrees or on horizontal branches encourages earlier fruiting than growing them in a bush shape, but special and regular pruning is needed.

Experiments with apple trees indicate that an unpruned tree will bear fruit long before one that is pruned and trained to form a framework of branches, but if trees are neglected and left unpruned for long, the quality, quantity and size of the fruit declines rapidly. The bush or tree becomes cluttered with branches and shoots, each intruding upon its neighbour's space and preventing the entry of light and air. Pests and diseases are also encouraged by a conglomeration of shoots. Pruning in the plant's early years is designed to create a framework of well-spaced, stout branches. Once this has been achieved, the emphasis changes to the regular production of fruit.

Other reasons for pruning fruit trees are to control the plant's vigour (which may be necessary with apple and pear trees), to remove pest- and disease-damaged shoots, to thin out clusters of fruit spurs and to counteract the tendency of some trees to bear more fruit one year than in the following one, a characteristic that is widely known as biennial bearing. If cordon, espalier and fan-trained trees are neglected for a few years, it may be impossible to return them to their earlier and more tidy shape.

With all fruit trees it is essential to begin to prune them soon after they are planted. There is no substitute for careful pruning in a plant's formative period, and for this reason this

Above: An apple tree trained into stepover formation, which is a variation of the espalier.
Left: Apple blossom is a welcome sign of spring.

topic is covered for all the types described here (see pages 92–3).

Pruning established fruit trees mainly involves the use of secateurs, but if the tree is excessively large and unfruitful other techniques have to be employed. These include bark-ringing and root-pruning, which are both old methods but still usable for tackling a large, unproductive tree. Nicking and notching is another unusual practice but ideal for use on cordon and espalier apple trees trained against a wall. It is used to encourage or deter the development of shoots and to make sure they grow in the right direction. These and other special techniques appropriate to the most popular fruit-bearing trees grown in temperate regions are explained and illustrated on the following pages.

apples & pears

Apples (*Malus domestica*) and pears (*Pyrus communis*) are the most popular tree fruits in temperate regions, each year reliably producing large crops. Because they flower before apples, the summer pruning of pears takes place about a week earlier than it does for apples. Otherwise, the pruning of both fruits is similar, although during a tree's formative period pears are best pruned less vigorously. Once they start to bear fruit, pear trees can be pruned more severely than apples, both when cutting back the tips of leading shoots and when shortening lateral ones. If thinning is neglected, the fruit will eventually be small and of poor quality.

Pruning apples and pears is an important operation and if performed wrongly may spoil the tree's shape and seriously delay the time when it begins to bear fruit. The initial purpose of pruning is to build up the shape or form of the tree, whether it is a bush, pyramid, cordon or espalier. Unless there is a strong, permanent framework of well-spaced branches, large crops of high-quality fruit cannot be produced. Creating a permanent framework may take four or five years if a maiden plant (one-year-old and with a single stem) is planted, but it is a task that cannot be rushed. The second purpose of pruning is to encourage the development of fruit buds and to regulate their number and positions.

In orchards, where these fruits are grown as bushes, half-standards and standards, they are pruned only in winter. In gardens, however, especially where they are grown as espaliers and cordons, they are pruned in both winter and summer. Occasionally, trees that are heavily pruned in summer become infested with woolly aphids (sometimes known as American blight). Winter pruning is normally carried out in a tree's dormant period, but it can be delayed and performed after buds begin to swell, although this often checks subsequent growth.

SUMMER PRUNING

Once a tree's framework and shape are established, specially trained trees, such as cordons and espaliers, can be summer pruned. The removal of shoots and leaves in summer checks the

Thinning fruits

Nature naturally regulates the number of fruits that apple trees bear, and in early summer fruitlets are usually shed. With some varieties, the fruitlets are thinned by the grower, who removes those that are misshapen or have been attacked by pests or diseases. This task is left until after the so-called midsummer 'drop', whereby a tree naturally discards fruitlets. Some varieties also shed fruit just before picking time; this is known as 'pre-harvest drop'.

growth of roots and reduces the development of shoots. It also leads to the formation of fruit buds at the base of the shoot that has been pruned.

WINTER PRUNING

This is performed in a tree's dormant period and has several purposes: to direct the growth of a tree into branch and shoot development; to prevent the overcrowding of branches and lateral shoots; and to regulate the number and position of fruit buds that subsequently develop and produce flowers and fruit.

ROOT-PRUNING

This is a way of encouraging apple trees that are growing too strongly to start bearing fruit. It should be tried only after other methods have failed. In late autumn and early winter, dig a trench 30–38cm (12–15in) deep in a complete circle 90–120cm (3–4ft) from the trunk. Sever all exposed roots, then refill and firm soil in the trench. For large trees, tackle this task over two winters.

NICKING AND NOTCHING

Nicking (**a**) is the removal of a piece of horseshoe-shaped bark immediately below a bud to reduce the flow of sap to it and prevent the bud's development. Notching (**b**) is where a piece of bark directly above a bud is removed, encouraging the bud to develop. Both nicking and notching are performed in late spring, when the sap is starting to flow, on apples and pears.

BARK-RINGING

This technique is used to encourage a vigorous tree to produce fruit rather than shoots. It is suitable only for use on apple trees and is regarded as a last resort to induce fruiting. Modern dwarf rootstocks have reduced the need for this technique, but it encourages more blossom to set and improves the quality of dessert varieties. Bark-ring trees at blossom time.

1 Use a sharp knife to cut just under the bark. Make two cuts, 6–12mm (¼–½in) apart. Make sure that they are parallel with each other and about 15cm (6in) below the lowest branch.

2 Remove the bark between the two cuts, making sure that the cut area is not widened. If it is too wide, there is a chance that the tree will be killed; if it is too narrow, it is ineffective.

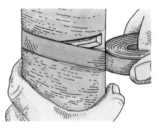

3 Do not paint the wound, but wind several layers of adhesive tape over the cut area. Once a callus has formed over the cut, the tape can be removed, usually by the latter part of midsummer.

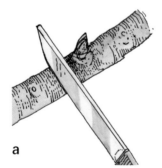

a

Use a sharp knife to make a horizontal cut, about 3mm (⅛in) deep and 6mm (¼in) below the bud. Then cut out a wedge shape by slicing towards it at a 45-degree angle. Carefully remove the small wedge of wood.

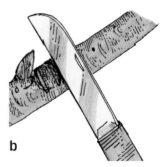

b

Use a sharp knife and make a 3mm (⅛in) deep cut 6mm (¼in) above the bud. Make a further cut, at a 45-degree angle, so that a wedge of wood can be removed. With both notching and nicking, do not damage the bud.

Left: Apples – here the variety is 'Michaelmas Red' – are among the most widely grown, hardy fruits.

formative pruning for apple & pear trees

Although it is possible to buy bush-trained trees that are two or even three years old, one-year-old plants, known as maidens, can be bought and trained. For this reason, formative training begins in the first winter with a maiden tree. Another term for these trees is 'whips', as they are formed of a single stem. In addition to buying and planting bare-rooted trees from late autumn to late winter, both one- and two-year-old trees can be bought growing in containers and planted at any time as long as the soil is not frozen or waterlogged.

1 From late autumn to late winter, plant bare-rooted one-year-old trees (maidens). These will have a single stem without any sideshoots. When two-year-old trees (sometimes known as feathered maidens) are planted, pruning begins as detailed in steps 3 and 4. Take care not to knock or excessively stain the graft or the area of the stem around it.

2 Prune the one-year-old tree in winter when it is dormant and whenever the air temperature is above freezing. When creating a dwarf bush shape, cut the stem back to 60cm (2ft) above the soil, severing just above a healthy bud. When an ordinary bush is being created, cut 75cm (2½ft) above soil level. Cutting the stem in this way stimulates growth.

3 By the following winter, the two-year-old plant will have developed several strong stems that grow upwards. Ideally, the bush should have shoots that form wide angles with the main stem, as these give a stronger joint than ones that form narrow angles and are close to the stem.

4 Select four of the strongest, healthiest shoots to form the main framework and cut them back by two-thirds. Make sure they are well spaced out. Prune each of them to just above a healthy, outward-facing bud. Also cut out all unwanted shoots flush with the main stem.

5 By the following winter, the three-year-old bush will have developed many shoots. Some will be extensions of the shoots pruned in the previous winter; others will arise from the trunk. The vigour of these stems depends on the previous season's pruning; if shoots were lightly tipped, subsequent extensions of them will be thin, pliable and unable to support heavy crops of fruit.

6 In winter, again cut back all leading shoots by about two-thirds of their length. Always cut them to just above an outward-pointing bud. Completely cut out damaged shoots, as well as those that cross the top of the bush. Small lateral shoots should be cut back to three buds long to encourage the formation of fruiting spurs. By this time the bush's head will be starting to form.

7 By the following winter, the four-year-old bush will have grown dramatically and will have several leading shoots and younger, slender sideshoots. The severity of winter pruning influences subsequent growth and development of fruit: the greater the proportion of wood removed, the more vigorous will be the following year's growth and the smaller will be the crop of fruit produced.

8 In winter, shorten the leading shoots by a third to a half, depending on the bush's vigour. Cut back lateral shoots that are growing on the insides of the branches and towards the bush's centre to about 10cm (4in) long. Prune out dead and crossing shoots. The early development of fruit can be encouraged by leaving some of the long, lower shoots unpruned.

Left: An established apple tree laden with fruit.

established apple & pear trees

Once an apple or pear tree is beyond its formative years (see pages 92–3), pruning assumes a different role. It is now done to encourage the formation of fruit buds and to make sure they are evenly positioned throughout the tree. There is also often a need to regulate a tree's vigour, although the choice of rootstock is the main means of controlling this. On very fertile soils trees can develop excessively vigorous growth. The first step to control this is to grass below the tree, depriving it of much of the nitrogen it was receiving and thereby reducing vegetative growth. Vigorous winter pruning encourages growth, and summer pruning is useful for curbing unproductive growth. Before winter pruning find out if the tree bears its fruit mainly on spurs or along the tip of shoots.

Apple varieties can be classified into two main types: spur-bearing types, which bear fruit mainly on fruit buds on short spurs that are close to the branch, and tip-bearing types, which produce fruit on fruit buds that are on or near the tips of shoots. Some varieties bear fruit in both of these styles. The technique for pruning apple and pear varieties with these characteristics differs.

Spur-fruiting dessert apples include: 'Ashmead Kernel', 'Cox's Orange Pippin', 'Discovery', 'Egremont Russet', 'Ellison's Orange', 'Golden Delicious', 'Idared', 'James Grieve', 'Kidd's Orange Red', 'Laxton's Fortune', 'Merton Knave', 'Orleans Reinette', 'Ribston Pippin', 'Sunset' and 'Tydeman's Late Orange'; culinary apples include 'George Neal', 'Grenadier', 'Howgate Wonder' and 'Lane's Prince Albert'.

Tip-bearing dessert varieties include: 'Beauty of Bath', 'Irish Peach' and 'Worcester Pearmain'.

Tip- or spur-bearing dessert varieties include: 'George Cave' and 'Lord Lambourne'; culinary varieties are: 'Bramley Seedling' and 'Golden Noble'.

Pear varieties can also be grouped according to where they bear their fruit, although most of the dessert types tend to develop them on spurs. The exceptions are 'Jargonelle' and 'Joséphine de Malines', which are tip-bearing.

Biennial bearing

Some apple varieties, such as 'Blenheim Orange', 'Bramley's Seedling' and 'Laxton's Superb', bear a heavier crop one year than another. One way to even out this problem is to take action in the spring, before a heavy crop is expected. Rub half to three-quarters of the fruit buds from each spur, leaving only one or two fruiting buds on each. Biennial bearing is less of a problem with pears.

Once a spur-bearing apple tree is established, the objective is to encourage the regular development of spurs along each branch. In winter, shorten lateral shoots to just above three or four buds from their bases. Also, shorten to one bud long laterals that were pruned the previous year. Prune back the leading shoot to half of the growth produced in the previous year.

Tip-bearing apple varieties bear most of their fruit towards the ends of shoots, so pruning aims to encourage the development of young shoots. For this reason, leave short lateral shoots unpruned, so that they develop fruit buds at their tips; they can be pruned back in later years. Some apple varieties bear fruit both on spurs and towards the tips of shoots; these

are best treated as spur-bearing types. Cut back leading shoots by about a third, severing them just above a healthy, upward-pointing bud. Leave all but the most vigorous lateral shoots unpruned, but cut back by half any that are more than 23cm (9in) long. The short laterals that are unpruned will develop fruit spurs. Cut back to one bud those shoots that are growing from laterals.

THINNING OUT SPURS

1 After several years branches of varieties that bear their fruit on spurs often become too numerous, forming complicated patterns. Because of the congestion, the quality and size of their fruit diminishes. This branch needs thinning.

2 In winter, thin out a few spurs and to remove others completely. Make sure that the remaining spurs are equally spaced. As well as concentrating the tree's energies into fewer spurs, more light and air can enter the tree.

SUMMER PRUNING

1 Summer pruning of apple and pear trees grown as bushes is not essential (unlike trained forms, such as cordons, espaliers and fans, for which it is a vital part of their training). However, it encourages the development of high-quality fruit and checks excessive growth. Cut back lateral shoots when their bases become woody, in late summer, to about 13cm (5in) from their bases.

2 If shoots are growing from the sideshoots, trim them to just above one leaf from their bases. Do not prune the leading shoot on each branch; it will be pruned later in winter. As well as improving the quality of the fruit, removing all this unneeded growth enables light and air to enter the tree to ripen the shoots and buds. It also improves the colour of the fruit.

Left: 'Ellison's Orange' apple trees grown as cordons.

apple & pear cordons

Apple and pear cordons are ideal in small gardens. They can be planted in the open garden or against a wall, but they need support from tiers of galvanized wires. The training and pruning information for growing apples and pears as both cordons and espaliers (see pages 98–9) starts with a one-year-old tree. This would have been grafted in the previous year. It is also possible to buy two- or three-year-old trees, but make sure they are properly shaped and have plenty of fruiting spurs. It is more difficult to match a partly trained tree to an existing framework of supporting wires than to start with a young plant. A young plant can also be transplanted more easily than one a few years older and becomes established far more quickly.

Cordons are formed of a single, straight stem, grown at an angle of 45 degrees and covered with spurs that bear fruit. Some cordons are grown vertically, but this is unusual as they grow higher and do not develop fruit as early as those planted obliquely. Some are grown with a single stem, others with two and, occasionally, three vertical branches.

Cordons are mostly pruned in summer, except in areas of high rainfall where masses of secondary shoots develop after summer pruning. It is best to winter prune neglected cordons initially, with a return to summer pruning later. As well as cutting back sideshoots to about 2.5cm (1in) of the main stem, thin out excessively long and tightly clustered spurs.

Pruning in winter is also a good way to stimulate a cordon's growth when it is failing to grow strongly enough.

Thinning spurs

The clusters of spurs on cordons eventually become congested and produce only small fruit. They can be thinned out at any time from late autumn to late winter. Use sharp secateurs to cut out buds that are weak and on the underside or markedly shaded by the branch. Thin out long, overlapping spurs to two or three fruit buds.

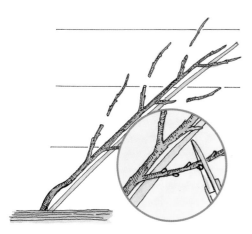

1 Plant maiden trees in the dormant season, from late autumn to late winter. They should be 75cm (2ft 6in) apart and at 45-degree angles by the side of tiers of supporting wires, 60cm (2ft), 1.2m (4ft) and 1.8m (6ft) above the ground. In addition, insert a 2.4m (8ft) long, strong bamboo cane slightly under the 45-degree stem. Tie the bamboo cane to the supporting wires, then the stem to the cane. Do not prune the leading shoot, but cut back laterals to within three or four buds of their base. Do not prune any that are shorter than this. Cut above a bud.

2 In the spring of the following year, leaves and blossom will begin to develop from the cut-back lateral shoots. Do not let cordons bear fruit in their first growing season. Remove the blossom but take care not to damage the growth bud just behind it. By midsummer of the same year young shoots will have developed from the cut-back laterals. These must be cut back to one leaf beyond the base cluster. Cut back to three leaves from their base all shoots growing directly from the main stem. Check that the stem is secure but not constricted.

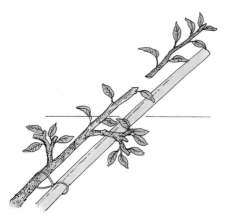

3 In late summer of the same year, just before the leaves fall off the plant, cut back further growth that has grown from shoots pruned back earlier. Prune it back to mature wood. High levels of rainfall often encourage the development of masses of secondary growth in late summer. If this happens repeatedly, resort to winter pruning. At this stage, do not cut back the leading shoot. In late spring of the following year, cut back the leading shoot when it has passed the top wire. At this stage, the cordon's top will be about 2.1m (7ft) high.

4 When the cordon is established, in midsummer of each year cut back the leading shoot to leave about 2.5cm (1in) of new growth. Also, prune back all mature lateral shoots that are growing from the main stem and are longer than 23cm (9in) to three leaves from their points of origin. Cut back shoots that are growing from existing spurs and sideshoots to one leaf beyond the rosette of leaves at their base. Do not include leaves that form a basal cluster in this number. Check that the main stem is firmly, but not too tightly, secured.

Left: A pear tree grown as an espalier – ideal for the small garden as it will take up very little space.

apple & pear espaliers

An espalier fruit tree needs to be supported on galvanized wires, strained between strong posts. Such a tree takes longer to create than a cordon, but it is an ideal way to grow apples and pears in a small garden. The tree is formed of a central stem, from which rise tiers of horizontal stems 38–45cm (15–18in) apart.

Build up the tiers in a systematic manner, as described here. As well as making sure that each tier is formed, build up fruiting spurs on the lower ones by cutting back laterals to three leaves above the base cluster. On the tier below that, cut back sub-laterals to one leaf.

If, in summer, one side of a tier is growing faster than the other one, lower it slightly. Conversely, if it is much smaller than its twin, raise it.

Once the tiers are formed and their ends have been cut back to fit the allotted space, prune them in the same way as for cordons (see pages 96–7). If an espalier is neglected for several years, it may be impossible to return it to its earlier, more tidy shape.

Rootstocks

There are several apple rootstocks used for both cordons and espaliers, but in a small garden M9 is best. For pears, Quince A or C rootstocks are suitable.

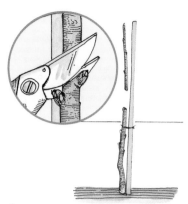

1 To create an espalier, plant a maiden apple or pear tree in winter. Cut back the stem to a healthy bud just above the bottom wire. In addition, there should be two other healthy buds positioned immediately below it.

2 The top three buds will grow from early to late summer. Loosely but firmly tie the leading shoots to a vertical cane, and the two sideshoots to two others at angles of 45 degrees. The canes are tied to the wires.

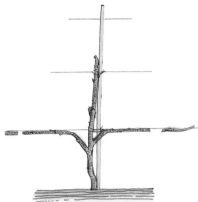

3 In the following winter, cut off the leading shoot just above the next wire. Shoots will develop to form the next tier. Lower the two side branches and shorten them by a third to a healthy, strong, downward-pointing bud.

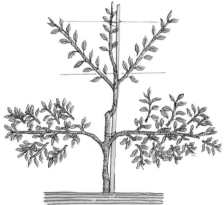

4 In summer, secure the leading and two top sideshoots to canes. Cut off shoots growing between the first and second tier to three leaves long. Prune sideshoots on the bottom tier to three or four leaves long.

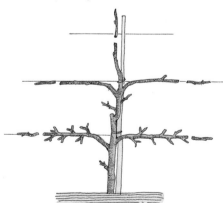

5 In subsequent winters, form further tiers in the same way as detailed earlier. Lower the tier created in summer and cut it back by a third. Also, tip back the shoots on the lower tier.

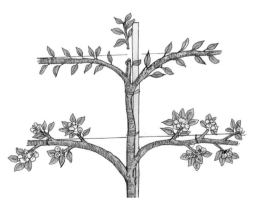

6 In early summer, when the top wire is reached, cut off the leading shoot. When the arms fill the wires, cut off their ends. Cut back sideshoots to three leaves and sub-laterals to one leaf.

Left: Plums need a warm, sheltered site to grow successfully.

plums & greengages

Once established, plums and greengages (*Prunus domestica*) grown as bushes, pyramids and half-standards require little pruning, although dead, crossing and rubbing branches should be removed every spring. Plums and greengages are not suitable for growing as espaliers and cordons, although they are often cultivated as fan-trained trees against a warm wall. When grown as fans, their training and pruning for the first few years is the same as for fan-trained peaches (see pages 104–5).

Thereafter, in spring rub out shoots growing towards the wall and in midsummer pinch out the tips of young shoots not required for the framework; they later become fruiting spurs. After cropping, cut the pinched-back shoots to three leaves.

PRUNING A BUSH PLUM

Begin by planting a two-year-old (feathered maiden) tree in late autumn or early winter. Do not plant it in late winter as growth often begins in early spring.

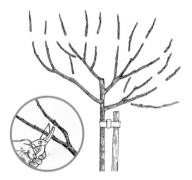

1 Start pruning a bush plum in late winter or early spring when growth begins and the buds start to break. Cut the central stem about 90cm (3ft) above the ground and slightly above a sideshoot. There should be three strong shoots below it. With each of these main shoots, prune them back by half to two-thirds, severing them just above an outward-facing bud. Then cut off, flush with the main stem, all sideshoots below the top four shoots.

2 In early spring of the following year, prune the bush, which will be three years old. The lateral shoots that were pruned back in the previous year will have produced extension growths. Prune these back by about half. At the same time, cut out at their bases all other shoots growing from the main shoots. At this stage, the bush will have about eight, well-spaced and strong stems. In the following years, little pruning is needed, other than cutting out dead or crossing branches in summer. Remove suckers from the ground and cut off shoots that are growing from the trunk and below the lowest main branch. Regularly check that the bush is securely staked.

PRUNING A PYRAMID TREE

This technique is designed to produce a framework of branches that will eventually form a pyramid 1.8–2.1m (6–7ft) high and about 1.2m (4ft) wide, which can be accommodated in many gardens and does not need supporting wires.

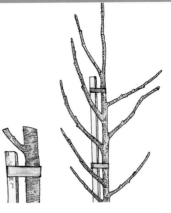

1 Pyramid trees differ from bush shapes in producing sideshoots (laterals) over a much longer part of the trunk. Plant a dormant, two-year-old tree (feathered maiden) in late autumn or early winter. Use tree-ties to secure the stem.

2 In late winter or early spring, cut back the leading shoot to 1.5m (5ft) above the ground. Cut out close to the main stem all lateral shoots within 45cm (18in) of the ground. This leaves the lateral shoots that will form the tree's main branches and framework. Prune back each of these shoots by half, cutting to a downward-pointing bud.

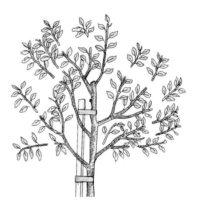

3 In the latter part of midsummer of the same year, shorten the current season's growth to 20cm (8in) long and a downward-pointing bud. Also, cut back sideshoots to 15cm (6in) long. Do not prune the leading shoot.

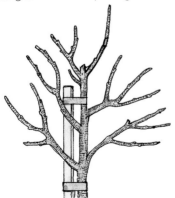

4 In early spring, prune the central shoot by about two-thirds of the growth produced in the previous summer. Repeat this in the following spring until the stem has reached the desired height. Thereafter, cut back the leading shoot by 2.5cm (1in).

5 In the latter part of midsummer of the same year, shorten the current season's growth on each of the leading shoots to eight leaves from its point of origin. Prune back lateral shoots to leave six leaves. Cut out vigorous shoots at the top of the tree.

Left: Nectarines (here the variety 'Pineapple') and peaches are closely related and are pruned in the same way.

peaches & nectarines

These two succulent fruits are closely related, and both are cousins of the almond. Nectarines (*Prunus persica* var. *nectarina*) are simply smooth-skinned forms of the peach (*P. persica*), slightly smaller and often considered to have a better, sweeter flavour. They respond to the same growing and pruning techniques, but nectarines are slightly less hardy than peaches. As well as being grown as bushes (described here), these fruits are frequently grown as fans against a warm wall (see pages 104–5). The yield of fruit varies widely and much depends on the weather and the size of the tree.

Peaches and nectarines bear fruit on shoots produced in the previous season, and it is essential throughout each year of the bush's life to encourage the development of new shoots to replace those that have borne fruit. There are three distinctive types of buds on peaches and nectarines: fruit buds, which are plump and develop fruit; growth buds, which are pointed and produce shoots; and triple buds, which have a plump, central fruit bud with growth buds on either side. It is important to prune shoots back to a growth bud when the development of a young shoot is desired. However, if a growth bud is not present, prune back to a triple bud.

Thinning congested fruit

In the first year, remove all blossom to make sure that the plant's energies are totally directed towards developing a strong framework. In the second year, leave the blossom intact but allow only a few fruits to mature. In all subsequent years the fruit must be thinned. This is especially important when peaches and nectarines are being grown on fan-trained trees against a wall. This is performed from early to midsummer. If it is not done the fruits do not grow to their full size. Start thinning the fruit when they are the size of large peas and stop when they reach the size of walnuts. First, reduce the pea-sized fruits to singles, eventually spacing peaches 23cm (9in) apart and nectarines 15cm (6in). On bushes they can be left slightly closer.

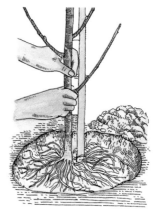

1 From late autumn to midwinter, plant two-year-old bush peaches and nectarines. Stake the tree and firm soil over the roots. As a bush, the tree will spread to 3.6–4.5m (12–15ft), so, although it benefits from the protection of a wall, do not plant it too close. Late spring frosts and cold winds can be very damaging.

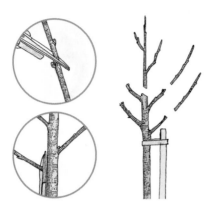

2 In early spring of the following year, when the buds start to grow, cut back the leading shoot to 75–90cm (2½ft–3ft) high and slightly above a strong lateral shoot. The head is formed of three or four lateral shoots; cut each back by two-thirds to an outward-facing bud. Cut off all other laterals close to the main stem. This initial pruning will form a head of well-spaced branches. Make sure that selected laterals are strong and healthy because if, at a later date, one has to be removed it will upset the bush's balance.

3 In the subsequent summer, young shoots will develop from the four main laterals that were cut back in early spring. Do not prune these in summer. Cut out to their bases shoots that are growing from them and towards the bush's centre. If left, they cause congestion. In addition, cut off, flush with the main stem, shoots that are growing below the main framework.

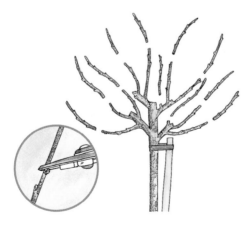

4 In early spring of the following year, cut back by half the young shoots. Sever them just above a healthy, outward-facing bud. Cutting back shoots in this way ensures the development of a strong framework of branches. Cut back sub-laterals to about 10cm (4in) from their base. In addition, cut out shoots that cross and crowd the bush's centre, as well as those that rub against each other and might subsequently cause damage through which diseases could enter the bush. The aim must be to make sure it has an open centre and that young branches are allowed to develop to replace those that are pulled down each year under the weight of fruit and have to be cut out.

5 By early to midsummer of the following year, the tree will be clothed in leaves and shoots that have developed from the cut-back shoots. Cut to their bases old shoots, those that cross the bush's centre and those that cause congestion and prevent the circulation of air and entry of light. In summer carefully use sharp secateurs to remove a few of the shoots that have borne fruit.

Left: Peach and nectarine fruits are borne on lateral shoots.

fan-trained peach & nectarine trees

Peaches and nectarines can be grown as fan-trained trees against warm, sunny walls. These fruits can also be grown against a wooden fence, but, as the lifespan of the fan is often more than that of a wooden fence, a brick wall is always a better choice. The objective with a fan-trained tree is to cover the space with branches that radiate from the tree's base, so that each branch receives the maximum amount of light and air. Building up the fan's framework is a long task. It is essential to create the fan from the base upwards, so that the central area is the last part to be filled.

Unlike many apple varieties, which have a long storage life, peaches and nectarines will keep for only about a week after being picked. It is often better to grow a fan-trained tree that requires little garden space and produces only 13.5kg (30lb) of fruit than a bush form, which can yield up to three times this amount and takes up vastly more room. A bush peach or nectarine is easier to grow than a fan-trained tree, but there is little point in producing a large crop of fruit if there are too many to eat after being harvested.

1 To create a fan-trained peach or nectarine tree plant a two-year-old tree (or feathered maiden) between late autumn and midwinter. Position it about 20cm (8in) from a wall. In late winter, cut back the main stem to about 60cm (2ft) above the ground and slightly above a strong lateral. Also cut back all other laterals to one bud from their bases. In early summer, a few shoots will have formed: remove all but the top one and two others, lower down and opposite each other.

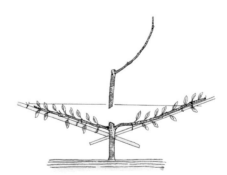

2 In the latter part of midsummer, use sharp secateurs to cut off the central stem and then tie the two arms at the plant's base to individual canes. These canes are tied to the supporting wires, with the stems loosely but securely tied to them. After the central stem has been cut out, apply a fungicidal paint to prevent diseases from entering the plant. Create the base of a fan before building up its centre. If one arm of the fan is not growing strongly, do not lower it as far as the other one.

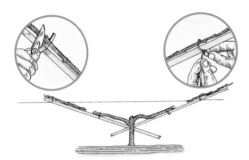

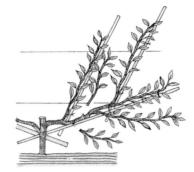

3 In early spring of the following year, cut back the two arms to a growth bud (sometimes known as a wood bud and identified as small and pointed) or a triple bud (two growth buds either side of a fruiting bud). Cut the stems 30–45cm (12–15in) from the main central stem.

4 Young shoots will develop along the arms. Select four strong shoots on each arm. Cut off all other sideshoots but leave one leaf at the base of each. For each shoot, tie a strong bamboo cane to the tiers of wires, then secure the shoot to it. Spread out the canes so that the shoots are equally spaced.

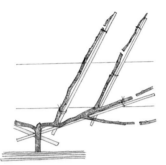

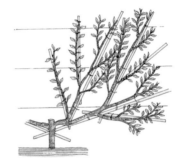

5 In early spring of the following year, cut back the new growth on each of these eight shoots by about a third. Make these cuts slightly above a downward-pointing growth bud.

6 In summer, let the shoot ends grow naturally. Allow three new shoots to develop on each arm, then tie them in, equally spaced. Rub out buds growing towards the wall. Allow shoots to grow every 10cm (4in) along the upper and lower sides.

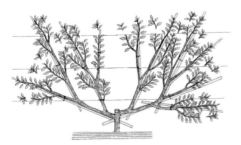

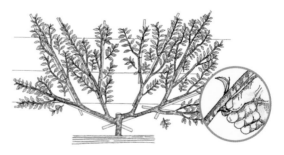

7 In late summer, when the lateral shoots that were selected earlier in the year are 45cm (18in) long, nip out their growing points. These are the young shoots that will bear fruit in the following year. Each year it is essential to encourage the development of fresh shoots that will bear fruit. If this is neglected, the yearly crop rapidly diminishes.

8 In late spring and summer every year, remove shoots growing towards and away from the wall. Young shoots produced during the previous year will bear fruit in the current season and should bear blossom and young sideshoots by early summer. Choose one at the side, another in the middle and one at the tip to extend the fruit-bearing lateral. Pinch back the remaining sideshoots to two leaves from their bases. After harvesting, cut back each fruited lateral to the replacement shoot at its base.

cherries

Cherries have been popular for many centuries: cherry orchards were known in England in the 1500s, while in 1833 an American fruit book notes nearly 50 varieties. Sweet and acid cherries are popular summer fruits – to many people they are the epitome of a country garden. Sweet cherries are more vigorous than acid ones, so are best reserved for large gardens or orchards. Acid cherries are better suited to small gardens.

Sweet cherries, which are also known as dessert cherries, are a favourite fruit. They are derived from *Prunus avium*, with white flowers in spring and fruit that ranges in colour from yellow and pink to black in the latter part of early summer until midsummer. Good varieties to consider growing include 'Early Rivers' (deep red flesh), 'Governor Wood' (dark red with yellow flesh), 'Merton Bigarreau' (black) and 'Van' (red).

Acid cherries have a different heritage from the sweet types, and the fruits are smaller. The trees are less vigorous than those of sweet cherries. They are derived from *Prunus cerasus*, with fruits that ripen from mid- to late summer. The fruits are tart, however, and when eaten raw are not to everyone's taste. They are often used in preserves and for other culinary purposes. Varieties to consider include 'Morello' (dark red) and 'Kentish Red' (scarlet, with yellow flesh).

Unlike the sweet cherries, which bear fruits on spurs on two-year-old and older wood, acid cherries develop most of their fruit on one-year-old shoots produced in the previous year. Therefore there is a need to make sure that fresh shoots are produced each year to replace those that have fruited and been cut out. The aim is to restrict excessive vegetative growth and to encourage the formation of fruit buds.

The duke cherry is a cross between the sweet and acid types, but is pruned in the same way as the sweet cherries.

Picking cherries

Leave the fruits on the tree until they are fully ripe. If, however, they start cracking, pick them immediately. Sweet cherries can be eaten raw; acid types are best used for cooking or in conserves. If the fruits are to be frozen, pick them while still firm. When picking the fruit, use sharp scissors to cut each stalk close to the shoot. If the cherry stalks are pulled off, the bark may be damaged, which can encourage the entry of diseases such as bacterial canker. Place the picked fruits in a basket, taking care not to bruise them.

PRUNING AN ACID CHERRY TREE

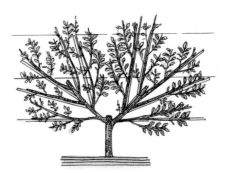

1 The pruning of a fan-trained acid cherry for the first three years is exactly the same as recommended for a fan-trained peach tree (see pages 104–5) as far as the planting, initial pruning and the first three years of growth are concerned, when the aim is to encourage the build-up of the fan-shaped framework, with evenly spaced ribs.

2 In the third year, allow the leading shoots on each rib to create extension growth. Tie these shoots to strong canes that are firmly secured to the wires.

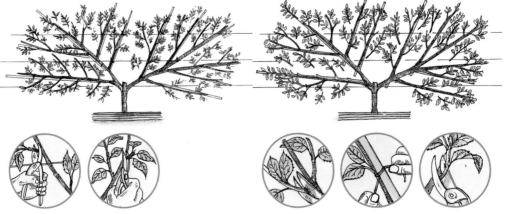

3 In late spring of the fourth and all subsequent years, thin out new shoots to 10–15cm (4–6in) apart and tie them to the wires while the shoots are still flexible enough. Leave a replacement shoot at the base of each lateral that will bear fruit. Cut out at their base all shoots that point directly at the wall. Allow the ends of the young shoots to grow naturally, where there is room, to clothe the wall with growth.

4 After the fan has borne fruit in the fourth year and subsequent years, cut out lateral shoots that have borne fruit to the young replacement shoot that was left when pruning in spring. Cut out shoots that have developed in summer and are pointing either towards the wall or directly away from it. Inspect all shoots to make sure that they are tied to the canes and wires. It is essential that the shoots cannot be blown about by the wind.

Left: A young fan-trained 'Morello' cherry.

fan-trained cherry trees

Sweet cherries need a warm, fairly sheltered site if they are to produce a good crop of fruit. They need sufficient space to achieve their full potential; height and spread can reach 7.5m (25ft). Make sure you get a self-fertile cultivar if you have room for only one plant.

Rootstocks

The rootstock determines the ultimate size of the tree and the shapes into which it can be trained. 'Colt' is a semi-dwarfing rootstock giving a height and spread of 5m (16ft). 'Inmil' is a dwarfing rootstock to 3.5m (12ft). Both can be used for bush, espalier, pyramid, spindlebush and fan shapes.

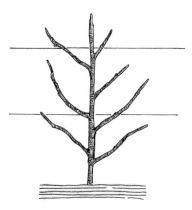

1 Plant a bare-rooted two-year-old tree (feathered maiden) in its dormant period, from late autumn to early spring. Container-grown trees can be planted at any time when the soil is neither frozen nor waterlogged. Plant the tree alongside tiered wires, about 23cm (9in) apart, from 30cm (12in) above the ground to about 2.1m (7ft) high.

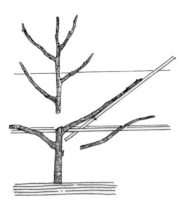

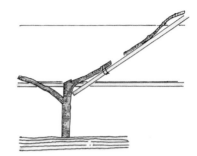

2 In the following spring, select two strong sideshoots near the base and use sharp secateurs to cut off the central stem, just above the top one. Tie the sideshoots to two canes, then to the wires.

3 In spring of the following year, cut each lateral shoot to about 30cm (12in) from the central stem. Cut them slightly above an outward-pointing bud. This severe pruning encourages the development of a strong framework.

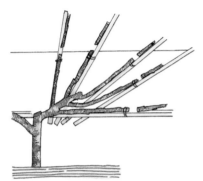

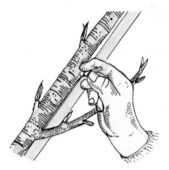

4 In summer, shoots grow from the two arms. Tie them to canes and train them into position. In the spring, cut them back to outward-pointing buds, leaving 45–50cm (18–20in) of new growth.

5 In the following spring and subsequent ones, rub out young shoots that are growing outwards or directly towards the wall. This is also a way to make sure that shoots are equally spaced.

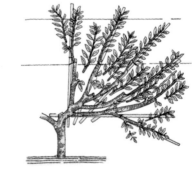

6 In the latter part of midsummer of the same year, cut back to five or six leaves all shoots that are not needed to extend or build up the framework. Also tie in sideshoots that are required to fill up bare areas or to replace old wood. Eventually, shoots will reach the top of the wall; then cut them back to a weak lateral shoot.

7 By the end of early autumn, the shoots will have grown further but their growth will be slowing down. Use sharp secateurs to cut back to three leaves of their bases all lateral shoots that were cut back in midsummer. This will encourage the development of fruit buds at their base in the following year. Make sure that the fan's roots do not become dry during summer as this will affect the development of young, healthy, new shoots.

figs & mulberries

These unusual fruits deserve to be more widely grown. Once, they were once better known: the Romans are said to have planted figs throughout Europe, and both fruits were widely featured in North American books on fruit in the early 1800s. Figs are chiefly known for their succulent fruits, which can be eaten fresh or dried. In the past the leaves were used in the East in preserving embalmed bodies, and green branches and leaves were boiled down to produce a deep golden dye. The leaves on their own produce a deep yellow stain, with a fragrance that remains in the cloth even after several washings. The fruits are also used to make a well-known laxative. The black mulberry also has a medicinal value, forming a syrup to soothe sore throats.

Figs (*Ficus carica*) do grow in warm areas in temperate countries, bearing fruits on the tips of well-ripened shoots produced the previous summer. Second crops may develop on shoots produced earlier in the year, but these seldom ripen in temperate countries and are best removed in early autumn. In cooler areas they are best grown as fan-trained trees against a warm, sheltered wall. Fruits ripen between late summer and mid-autumn, and as the stalk softens they hang down. If figs become too rampant, their growth can be controlled by root-pruning.

The common or black mulberry (*Morus nigra*) probably comes from Asia but has for many years been established in Europe and North America. The juicy fruits are picked once they ripen in late summer. The mulberry forms a large, slow-growing tree, which takes about eight years to bear fruit. Little pruning is needed; cuts are likely to bleed and must be cauterized with a hot poker. Prune only fully dormant plants in winter – young ones to create a framework of four or five branches and afterwards to remove dead or misplaced branches.

The white mulberry (*M. alba*) has sweet but insipid, white, pink or purplish fruits, and is mainly grown for its light-green leaves, so beloved by silkworms.

Restricting fig roots

The roots of fig trees must be constrained to prevent them from producing masses of leafy growth and few fruits. Prepare the planting area by digging a hole 60cm (2ft) square and deep. Line it with bricks or paving slabs and fill with 30cm (12in) of rubble. Then fill with soil with added rubble.

FAN-TRAINING A FIG

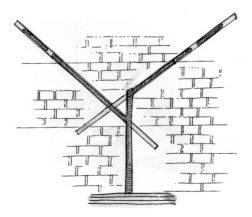

1 In winter, plant a two-year-old container-grown fig tree in the shelter of a warm wall, 15–20cm (6–5in) away from its base. Position the plant about 10cm (4in) deeper than before. Erect supporting wires, 23cm (9in) apart, from 45cm (18in) above the ground to the top of the wall. In spring, cut back the central stem to just above the lowest wire and immediately above a lateral shoot. Select two shoots to form the arms and tie them to canes secured at 45 degrees to the wires. Cut back both arms to a bud 45cm (18in) from the trunk. Cut off other laterals.

2 In the following summer, allow four shoots to grow from each of the two arms: one at the end of the arm to form extension growth, one from the underside and two on the top side. Rub out all other buds growing from the arms and secure the eight shoots to bamboo canes. The objective at this stage is to form a strong framework of branches that are spaced out so that light and air can enter the fan. Allow plenty of space between the newly formed ribs because fig leaves are large and create a great deal of shade.

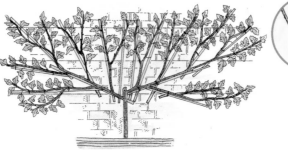

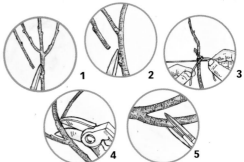

3 In late winter of the following year, prune back each of the main shoots, cutting slightly above a bud, which will continue its growth in the desired direction; leave about 60cm (2ft) of the previous season's growth. In summer, allow further shoots to develop. Rub out unwanted buds.

4 It often takes four years to create a framework of evenly spaced ribs on the fan. Once this has been achieved, the routine is to prune the fan in spring and again in summer. (**1**) In spring, use sharp secateurs to cut out diseased and frost-damaged shoots. (**2**) Thin out young shoots to just above one bud from their base. (**3**) Position and tie in young shoots. (**4**) Completely remove shoots growing towards and away from the wall. (**5**) Cut out some of the old, bare shoots to slightly above the first bud from its base. In early summer, cut back young growths to five leaves from their base.

grape vines

The techniques of pruning grape vines are many and varied. Grape vines grown in greenhouses in temperate countries have individual needs, which are often dictated by the limited height of the structure.

A popular pruning method is the 'single cordon', which is described here, and it is generally regarded as the best solution for outdoor cultivation. Variations on it include the 'double cordon' (two vertical shoots trained from a single rod) and 'multi-cordon' (four vertical shoots trained from a single rod). Whichever method is used, it is based on the vine's fruiting nature: fruit is borne on one-year-old stems. Grape vines should, therefore, be pruned each year to encourage the development of young lateral shoots that will bear fruit. In summer the laterals are pruned back to concentrate the vine's activities into developing fruits on them.

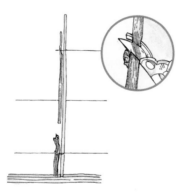

1 Plant a bare-rooted grape vine in early spring. Firm the soil and erect tiers of galvanized wires, spaced 30cm (12in) apart and held 13cm (5in) away from a warm wall. Position the bottom wire 45cm (18in) above the ground. Immediately after planting cut the main stem to slightly above a strong bud and about 50cm (20in) high. Prune all others to a single bud from their base. Tie the rod to a cane.

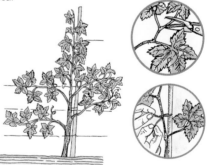

2 In the following summer, a shoot will grow from a bud at the top of the main stem, as well as from buds lower down. Train the central shoot upwards and tie it to a bamboo cane secured to the wires. In midsummer, cut back all lateral shoots (those growing directly from the main stem) to just beyond five or six leaves. Cut back to just above one leaf all shoots that are growing from the laterals. In addition, totally cut back to the stem any shoots that are growing from the base of the main stem.

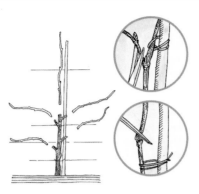

3 Next winter, when the vine is dormant cut back the leading shoot, leaving a third of the previous season's growth. Cut back lateral shoots to leave just one strong bud at the base of young shoots produced the previous year. Check the central shoot is secured to the cane but not constricted.

4 In summer, when the laterals have developed nine or ten leaves, cut them back to five or six leaves from their base. Pinch sub-laterals back to just above one leaf from their base. Pinch out flower trusses that form on the laterals. Early crops of grapes should be avoided.

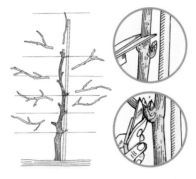

5 Between early and midwinter, cut back the leading shoot to leave a third of the young, growth produced in the previous summer. Sever the shoot just above a strong bud and cut back lateral shoots to leave one bud on the new growth.

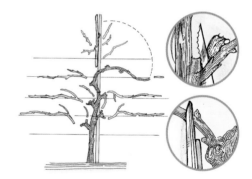

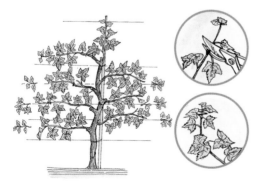

6 By the following summer, the vine will be growing strongly. Cut back laterals with a flower truss to two leaves beyond the fruiting cluster. Laterals not bearing fruit should have their tips pruned to just beyond five or six leaves. On weak lateral shoots, pinch out all but one flower truss. Pinch back shoots developing from laterals to one leaf.

7 Between early and midwinter, prune the vine again. Prune lateral shoots by cutting them back to the first strong bud on the growth produced in the previous year. If the leading shoot has not reached the top supporting wire, cut it back to leave a third of the previous season's growth. However, when it reaches the top, cut it back to leave just two buds on the new growth. From then on, cut it back to two new buds each year. Also, at that stage, sever the ties from the top half of its length and lower it to a near horizontal position for a few weeks. This encourages the even development of shoots along its length. In spring, re-tie the shoot in a vertical position. Eventually, spurs at the base of lateral shoots become congested. If this happens, use a small saw to remove them.

7 SOFT FRUIT

Even the smallest garden can usually
accommodate a small currant bush or a few
canes of raspberries, and if varieties are chosen
with care it is possible to have fresh fruit over a
long period from summer until the first frosts. All
these fruits require regular attention, but they will
more than repay the work involved in their annual
pruning with abundant crops.

Above: Fan-trained redcurrants are ideal fruits to grow in small gardens.
Left: Gooseberries growing among colourful perennials in a cottage garden.

Bush fruits, such as gooseberries, blackcurrants, redcurrants and whitecurrants, have different habits of growth. Some of these bear fruit mainly on shoots produced from the plant's base in the previous year; others have a more permanent framework. All, however, need regular pruning, because if they are neglected they soon become a jungle of shoots, and this is accompanied by a rapid decline in the quality and quantity of fruit they bear. Blackcurrant bushes are especially prone to becoming congested when they are left untended, quickly producing a mass of old, unfruitful stems. Cane fruits, such as raspberries and some of the more vigorous hybrid berries, become a mixture of old and fruited shoots and weak, spindly new ones. The yearly removal of old canes encourages the development of young, healthy ones.

Blueberries and cranberries are hardy shrubs that need acid soil to ensure their survival. The highbush blueberry (*Vaccinium corymbosum*) is native to North America and popular in blueberry

pie, although the juicy fruits can also be eaten stewed with sugar. Cranberries (*V. oxycoccos*) are also native to America, as well as Europe. The fruit is used in cranberry sauce and served with turkey and venison. In addition, there are several related shrubby plants that yield edible berries, although they are infrequently grown in fruit gardens. These include bildberries (*V. myrtillus*, also known as bilberries, blaeberries and whortleberries), lowbush blueberries (*V. angustifolium*) and large or American cranberries (*V. macrocarpon*).

The highbush blueberry is an ideal fruiting shrub in gardens with very acid soil, about pH 4.5. It so loves acid soil that it is likely to fail where the pH reading is above 5.5. For the first three years after planting no pruning is needed. After this period the aim is to stimulate fresh growth that will bear fruit two years later: this is because blueberries bear fruit on the tips of the previous season's shoots.

Cut out unproductive or weak shoots and encourage the

development of fresh, fruit-bearing shoots by completely cutting back a few of the oldest stems to their base. Completely prune out low-growing or downward-pointing branches. Try to keep the growth upwards.

Cranberries are also acid-loving plants, and are a close relative of the blueberry. They need little pruning, other than occasionally cutting out very old stems in spring and making sure that they do not encroach upon neighbouring plants. To keep plants bushy, use hand shears in mid-spring to snip off the ends of shoots. Rather than cutting off long shoots, they can be layered in autumn and encouraged to form roots. Sever rooted stems from the parent plant in the following autumn and re-plant them in spring.

Left: Cordon-trained redcurrants.

redcurrants & whitecurrants

Redcurrants and whitecurrants (*Ribes sativum*) are hardy deciduous shrubs, grown in temperate areas, and make ideal summer fruits for small gardens. They are pruned in the same way; blackcurrants are dealt with in a different way (see pages 118–19). Instead of forming 'stools' in the manner of blackcurrants, with new shoots developing from ground level or from previously pruned stems close to the plant's base, red- and whitecurrants grow on bushes with 'legs'. These are stems 15–20cm (6–8in) long that connect the roots with the branches. The branches should not arise from soil level.

Red- and whitecurrants produce fruit on short spurs that develop on the old wood, as well as in clusters at the base of young growths formed in the previous year. Like many other fruits, they need to be pruned in both winter and summer, especially when trained as cordons. Summer pruning helps to create fruiting spurs without encouraging the growth of shoots. Bush-grown types yield 3.5–4.5kg (8–10lb) of fruit, while single cordons should produce 1–1.3kg (2–3lb).

BUSH-GROWN RED- AND WHITECURRANTS

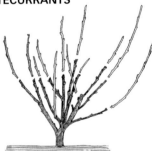

1 Plant one-year-old bushes in their dormant period, from late autumn to late winter. Plant the bush slightly lower than it was growing before. In winter, prune back all shoots by half, cutting to just above an outward-pointing bud. If two-year-old bushes are planted, this will reduce the time taken to produce fruit.

2 In the second dormant period, when the bush is two years old, prune each branch back by half to an outward-pointing bud. In the third dormant period cut all leading shoots back by 15cm (6in). Always cut the shoots to just above an outward-pointing bud. Cut back lateral shoots to about two buds from their bases.

3 In the fourth and subsequent years, cut back the leading shoots by only 2.5cm (1in) or even less. Continue to cut back lateral shoots to form new spurs and to remove old shoots from the plant's centre. Each year cut back new lateral shoots to about five leaves from their bases. Do not prune the leading shoots.

CORDON RED- AND WHITECURRANTS

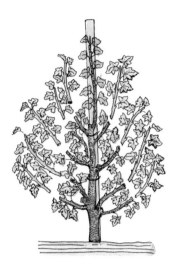

1 Plant one-year-old red- and whitecurrants in winter, 38cm (15in) apart. At this stage each plant will have a central stem and about four sideshoots. Immediately after planting, shorten the central shoot by a third to a half of its length, cutting to an outward-facing bud. Cut back lateral shoots to one bud from their base, but completely remove those within 10cm (4in) of the ground. Stake each plant.

2 In the following year, in early midsummer, prune back the current season's sideshoots to four or five leaves from their base. Do not prune the leading shoot at this stage but make sure that the new growth – as well as the previous season's wood – is tied to the supporting stake. Make sure that the ties do not strangle the shoots: securely tie the string to the stake, then loop it around a stem.

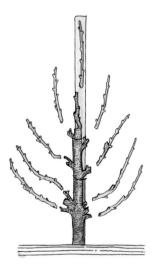

3 In the second and later years, you should prune cordons in winter. Cut back the leading shoot to slightly above a healthy bud and remove all but 15cm (6in) of the new growth. In subsequent years, cut back the leading shoot to leave only one bud of new growth. In addition, cut back to leave 2.5cm (1in) of new growth on all lateral shoots that were pruned in the previous summer. Pick up and burn any wood cut from the plants.

4 In the following and all subsequent summers, you should leave pruning the leading shoot until the winter, but need to cut back the sideshoots to leave only four or five leaves of the fresh growth that was produced earlier during the same season. Continue to tie the central, leading shoot to a support, but remember that during the following winter it will need to be cut back to leave only one bud of fresh growth.

Left: Blackcurrants produce their best fruit on shoots that have developed in the previous season.

blackcurrants

Blackcurrants (*Ribes nigrum*) are easily grown and pruned, and unlike redcurrants and whitecurrants they have to be grown as free-standing bushes.

They cannot be grown as espaliers or cordons. They can be planted at any time in their dormant period, from mid-autumn to early spring, as long as the ground is not frozen or waterlogged, and they will eventually form large bushes, with stems growing from soil level. Plants which are grown in this way – with new growth produced from ground level – are known as stools.

Blackcurrants produce their best fruit on shoots that have developed in the previous season, although some fruits are borne on older wood. The yearly cycle of pruning is designed to cut out much of the older wood that has borne fruit and to encourage the development of young shoots. Pruning in this way also helps to prevent the bush becoming congested with shoots.

Before planting, prepare the ground thoroughly, removing all perennial weeds and digging in plenty of manure. Blackcurrants need a sunny site, that is sheltered from strong winds.

Rejuvenating old bushes

When blackcurrant bushes are neglected they become a mass of old shoots that bear few and inferior fruits. If the bushes are especially old and full of dark wood, they are best pulled out and replanted with fresh, young plants. If the neglect has been for only three or four years, however, they can be rejuvenated by cutting all stems to their bases in late summer or early autumn. Drastic pruning such as this encourages the development of new shoots from ground level and the plant's base. However, it does mean that no fruit will be produced in the following year, when a mass of one-year-old shoots will be created.

To encourage the development of these young stems after cutting back in spring, sprinkle a general fertilizer around the bush, water thoroughly and add a mulch. In addition, in summer keep the soil moist and pull up any weeds growing around the plant's base.

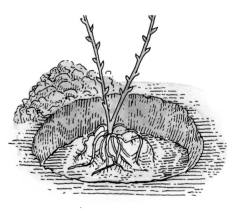

1 Plant young blackcurrant bushes in their dormant period, setting them slightly deeper than before; the old soil level mark will be visible on the stem.

2 Firm soil around and over the roots, then immediately cut back all stems to about 2.5cm (1in) above soil level. Although this may appear to be drastic, it encourages the development of fresh, young shoots from the plant's base in the following year. If this initial pruning is neglected, the quality and amount of fruit will be severely diminished.

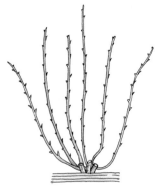

3 By the end of the following summer, young shoots will have developed, and by autumn, when the plant's leaves will have fallen off, these will resemble the plant shown here. No pruning is needed at this stage.

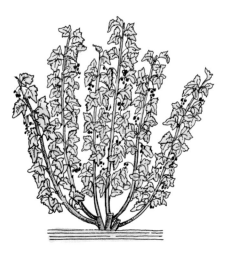

4 In the following year, these stems will bear fruit. At the same time fresh shoots will have developed from the bush's base, and these, too, will later bear a crop of fruit.

5 In all subsequent years, ideally prune the bush as soon as the fruit has been picked; if this is not possible, autumn is also suitable. Cut out old wood to its base. This will remove the majority of shoots that produced fruit in the current season. Cut out damaged and crossing shoots so that light and air can penetrate the bush to assist in the ripening of young shoots.

Blackcurrant varieties

Early-fruiting:
● *'Boskoop Giant' and 'Laxton's Giant'.*
Mid-season:
● *'Ben More', 'Ben Nevis' and 'Wellington XXX'.*
Late-fruiting:
● *'Ben Sarek' and 'Amos Black'.*

gooseberries

Above: Gooseberries are easy to grow, but they need cool conditions and regular mulching.

Unlike blackcurrants, which form a mass of stems from ground level, gooseberries (*Ribes uva-crispa*) develop a short stem, known as a 'leg', which supports the branches on which the fruits are borne. Most gooseberries are grown as bushes, but some can be trained as single, double or even triple cordons, as well as in fan shapes.

Gooseberry bushes – and other trained forms – bear fruits on one-year-old wood and spurs that develop from older shoots. On plants grown as cordons, the fruits are borne on spurs that develop directly from the main stem, and such plants create unusual and attractive features.

The initial pruning of bushes is directed towards creating a strong framework of permanent branches, evenly spaced around the main stem. Later pruning, for bushes and specially trained forms, involves cutting them in both winter and summer.

Gooseberry varieties

Early-fruiting:
- 'Broom Girl', 'Golden Drop' and 'May Duke'

Mid-season:
- 'Careless', 'Invicta', 'Keepsake' and 'Leveller'

Late-fruiting:
- 'Lancer', 'White Lion', 'Lancashire Lad' and 'Lord Derby'

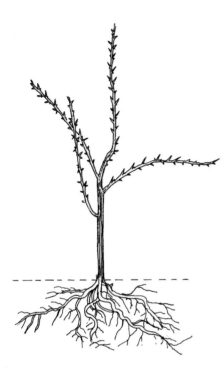

1 Plant a one-year-old (maiden) gooseberry bush in its dormant period, from late autumn to late winter. Set the plant firmly in the soil, only fractionally deeper than before, making sure it has a 'leg'.

2 Immediately after planting, prune back each main branch by a half, cutting to an upward-pointing bud. Make sure that the plant has a stem that is 15–20cm (6–8in) long.

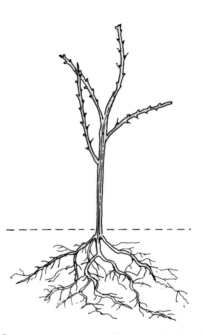

3 By late autumn or early winter of the following year, strong shoots will have developed from the cut-back stems. Shorten them back by a half to inward- and upward-pointing buds. By the following late autumn, further growth will have developed; shorten all leading shoots by a half. Shorten laterals to 5cm (2in) long and cut out crossing shoots.

4 In all subsequent years, in the latter part of early summer, prune all lateral shoots produced that season to five leaves. Do not prune leading shoots. In the following winter, cut back leading shoots by half and all lateral shoots to about two buds from their base.

raspberries

Raspberries (*Rubus idaeus*) are among the most popular and widely grown of all soft fruit, and the fact that it is possible to achieve yields of 2–3kg (5–6lb) for each 90cm (3ft) of row of summer-fruiting varieties and about 200g (8oz) for autumn-fruiting types makes them worthwhile additions to any garden. Growing both summer- and autumn-fruiting types means that it is possible to have fresh fruit from midsummer through to the frosts of autumn.

The single-post system is an easy way to support just a few canes in a small garden. Before planting the canes, insert posts 2.4m (8ft) long and 6cm (2¼in) thick into the ground to a depth of 60cm (2ft). The canes are later bunched around them and loosely tied with long loops of wire or strong string at intervals up the post.

The single-fence system is the normal method of supporting raspberry canes. At each end of the row insert strong posts, 2.4m (8ft) long, so that the tops are about 1.8m (6ft) above the ground. Stretch three lengths of galvanized wire between the posts so that the wires are 75cm (2½ft), 1m (3ft 3in) and 1.6m (5½ft) above the ground.

For the double-fence system, insert square-cut posts, 2.1m (7ft) long and 6cm (2½in) thick, into the ground at each end of a row so that the tops of the posts are 1.5–1.6m (5ft–5½ft) above the ground. Fix two battens, each 75cm (2½ft) long, horizontally and about 1m (3¼ft) apart, to the outer side of each post. Stretch strong, rust-resistant, galvanized wires between them, so that the plants are enclosed and supported within the wires.

Raspberry varieties

Summer fruiting:
● 'Glen Cova' and 'Glen Moy' (both early), 'Malling Admiral' and 'Malling Jewel' (both mid-summer) and 'Leo' (late)
Autumn fruiting:
● 'Heritage', 'Zeva' and 'Fallgold'

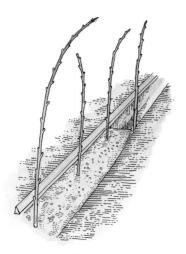

1 Plant summer-fruiting raspberry canes from late autumn to early spring 45cm (15in) apart and about 8cm (3in) deep in well-prepared soil. Spread out the roots and firm soil over them. Align the rows north to south so that one row does not excessively shade its neighbour, and if several rows are planted space them 1.8m (6ft) apart.

2 Immediately after the canes are planted, cut them down to 23–30cm (9–12in) high just above a healthy, dormant bud. While the canes are small is the time to erect tiers of strong supporting wires, 75cm (2½ft), 1m (3½ft) and 1.6m (5½ft) above the ground, on sturdy posts. In late winter re-firm any soil around the roots that has been loosened by frost.

3 In spring, young shoots that appear from ground level will bear fruit in the following year. Cut off the old, 23–30cm (9–12in) high canes above ground level. In the subsequent summer, tie the new canes to the supporting wires. Do not allow more than eight canes to develop, although in the first year it is unlikely that this number will form.

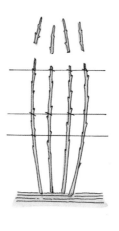

4 In late winter, use secateurs to cut off the tips of all canes, about 15cm (6in) above the top wire and slightly above a healthy bud. In the following summer, canes will develop that produce fruit in the following year. In each spring, this cycle of canes produced in the previous year and fresh shoots developing from the plant's base is repeated.

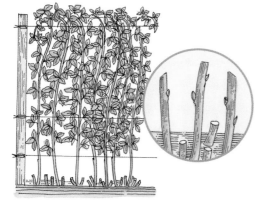

5 As soon as the fruits have been picked, cut down to their bases all the canes that produced fruit. This will leave the young canes that developed earlier in the same year and that will produce fruit in the following season. Do not allow more than eight to develop from each plant. Space them out and tie them to the wires so that they are about 10cm (4in) apart. If the young canes are strong and vigorous, tie their tips to the top wire to minimize further vigorous growth. This also encourages both the tip of the cane and the rest of it to mature rapidly and to ripen.

Left: Thornless blackberry cultivars are generally less vigorous than prickly ones.

blackberries, loganberries & hybrid berries

The cultivated forms of blackberry (*Rubus fruticosus*) are far plumper and sweeter than those gathered from hedgerows, and an established plant will yield 4.5–9kg (10–20lb) of fruit and sometimes as much 13.5kg (30lb). Varieties of blackberry include 'Bedford Giant' (vigorous, bright black fruits in mid- and late summer), 'Himalaya Giant' (medium-sized fruits in late summer) and 'Oregon Thornless' (this is a popular variety bearing thorn-free canes, which bear fruit in late summer and into early autumn).

Hybrid berries, such as tayberries, boysenberries and dewberries, have mainly evolved from crosses between blackberries and raspberries. Most hybrid berries are not as vigorous as blackberries. Loganberries, another hybrid, are said to have originated in California from a natural cross between a raspberry and a blackberry, which was spotted by Judge J.H. Logan more than a century ago. The rich red fruits are up to 5cm (2in) long and have a distinctive flavour. They are ready for picking in mid- and late summer. There are two clones: L654 (which is thornless) and LYS9 (thorned).

In addition to the weaving method illustrated here, blackberries, loganberries and other hybrid berries can be trained as fans along parallel, horizontal wires, and, although it requires a great deal of attention, the method produces a heavy crop. Sometimes the new canes are grown in among the old ones, but a variation is to grow all the old canes on one side and the new ones on the other. This makes pruning easier as the old, fruited stems can be easily identified. Use soft string to tie the canes to the wires, loosely but securely.

An alternative system, known as roping, involves tying the canes in groups of three or four to individual wires, and this is an easier and quicker system of training cane fruits than the fan method. Training the old and new canes on different sides of the plant makes pruning easier. Old fruited canes are cut off at their bases. In the following season, young canes will develop on the other side, and these are trained in small groups along the wires.

1 Plant blackberries and hybrid berries at any time from mid-autumn to late winter, whenever the soil is not frozen or waterlogged. Position the young plants about 1.8–3m (6–10ft) apart against a series of horizontal supporting wires. Vigorous varieties are better spaced 3.6m (12ft) apart. Each year the plants will produce young canes that bear fruit in the following season.

2 Immediately after planting, cut down each stem to about 23cm (9in) above the ground, severing the stem just above a healthy bud to encourage the development of young shoots from ground level. In early spring, re-firm soil over the plant's roots; severe frosts often disturb the soil and, unless re-firmed, this will retard a plant's subsequent growth.

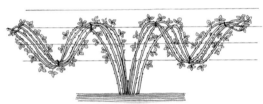

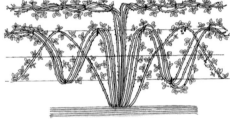

3 In the first summer, young canes grow from the plant's base. Weave and secure them between the lower three tiers of wires, spreading them equally on both sides. At this stage, the top wires are left bare, so that young canes produced in the following year can be trained along them.

4 In the following year, train in the new canes that developed from the plant's base. Loosely tie them in clusters so that air and light can penetrate among them. The circulation of air helps to prevent the onset of diseases. Do not allow the two seasons' canes to become mixed as this will cause problems later in the year.

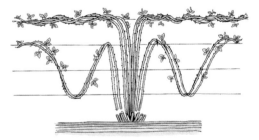

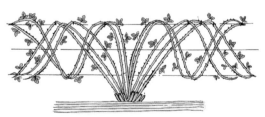

5 The old canes will start to bear fruit in late summer. As soon as fruiting is over, cut out to their bases all those canes that produced fruit. Sever the ties that secure them to the wires and burn both the ties and the old canes. Never try to compost them. Wear stout gloves while pruning and freeing these old canes from their supporting wires.

6 When all the old canes have been removed, untie from the top wire all the canes that were produced in the current year. These are the canes that will bear fruit in the following season. Light and air are essential at this stage to ripen the canes, so space them equally and not in clusters. In autumn, cut off the tips from weak and young canes. In late winter cut back the ends of shoots damaged by frost.

INDEX

ACKNOWLEDGEMENTS

Garden Picture Library/Linda Burgess 80 Bottom, /Zara McCalmont 50 Bottom, /Brian Carter 110, /Eric Crichton 78, 85, /John Glover 5 detail 5, 29, 65, 66, 74, 83, 87, 118, 120, /Neil Holmes 5 detail 7, 22, 124, /Lamontagne 43 Top, 82, /Jane Legate 39 Top, /Mayer/Le Scanff 48 Top, 94, 106, /Jerry Pavia 2–3, 73, /Laslo Puskas 30, /Howard Rice 37, 39 Bottom, 61, 70 left, 70 right, 72 right, 100, 102, /JS Sira 20, 40, /Brigitte Thomas 5 detail 4, 68, /Steve Wooster 46, 90,

Octopus Publishing Group Ltd./Michael Boys 5 detail 1, 12 left, 32, /Vana Haggerty Back Cover, /Jerry Harpur 7, 31, /Andrew Lawson Front Cover bottom, 63, 64, /Guy Ryecart 11 Bottom, /Howard Rice Front Cover top left, 5 detail 3, 23, 26, 34, 38, 53, 55 bottom, 76, 79, 86, 96, 98, 104, 108, 112, 116, 122, /Guy Ryecart 10 Top, 10 Centre Left, 10 Centre Right, 10 Bottom Left, 10 Bottom Right, 11 Top, 11 Top Centre, 11 Centre Left, 11 Centre Right, 11 centre right below, /Mark Winwood Front Cover top right, /Steve Wooster 5 detail 2, 5 detail 6, 8, 9, 13, 15, 28, 59, 84, 88, /George Wright 4–5, 16, 27 left, 56,

Harpur Garden Library 14, 16–17, 18 Top, 21, 27 right, 52, 54, 55 Top, 60, /Fudlers Hall, Essex 58,

Andrew Lawson 18 Bottom, 24, 41 Top, 41 Bottom, 42, 43 Bottom, 44, 48 Bottom, 50 Top, 57, 62, 72 left, 80 Top, 81, 92, 114, 115, /Bosvigo House Cornwall 75, /Old Rectory, Sudborough Northants. 89

Executive Editor: Julian Brown
Editorial Manager: Jane Birch
Designer: Les Needham
Picture Research: Christine Junemann
Production Controller: Ian Paton